Mother, mother ocean, I have heard you call
Wanted to sail upon your waters since I was three feet tall
You've seen it all, you've seen it all
Watched the men who rode you switch from sails to steam
And in your belly you hold the treasures few have ever seen
Most of them dream, most of them dream.

—*Jimmy Buffett*

WILDSAM PURSUITS

Places are endlessly complex: time, geography, culture and happenings layered with millions of stories. And often, one realizes that a place carries a specific heritage, a definitive pursuit that people build their lives around, a common trade or precious resource that might set the course for generations.

For the Gulf Coast, this pursuit is seafood.

A big thank-y'all goes to the chefs, restaurant owners and seafood industry workers who took time to talk to us during a time when pandemic-related stress was high. Special thanks to the brilliant journalists, writers and researchers with the *Tampa Bay Times*, *64 Parishes*, *Flamingo Magazine* and the Southern Foodways Alliance. Also, endless gratitude for the Southern Food and Beverage Museum's library. This book benefited from the insight of Michael Adno, Gabrielle Calise, Alyson Sheppard, Julian Rankin and many others. Thanks to Scott Hocker and Ladee Hubbard for writing special essays on hidden corners of the Gulf Coast. Let's all get a dozen on the half shell soon.

WILDSAM FIELD GUIDES™

Published in the United States
by Wildsam Field Guides, Austin, Texas.

ISBN 978-1-4671-9938-4

Illustrations by Jess Ruliffson

To find more field guides, please visit
www.wildsam.com

CONTENTS

*Discover the people and places
that tell the story of the Gulf Coast*

WELCOME

————

STANDING ON THE BEACH of what would become Florida in 1566, Spanish missionary Juan Rogel believed the Gulf Coast was his oyster. As historian Jack E. Davis puts it, Rogel held that God deemed man "the master of all on earth ... where he should reign as sovereign over the fish of the sea, the birds of the sky." The Calusa, the Indigenous people he planned to convert, believed when they died their spirits inhabited those birds and fish.

On a not-so-distant shore, Horn Island near Ocean Springs, Mississippi, some 400 years later, Walter Anderson, the Gulf's Gauguin, painted pelicans, redfish and crabs in lapis, lavender and lime. Once, he tied himself to a tree there to experience the awesome force of a hurricane first-hand. After, he wrote in his journal, "Why does man live? To be servant and slave of all the elements."

America's Sea has always embodied extremes, no more so than in its beauty and its wrath. The Gulf is a pitiless paradise. Just like the rise and fall of the tide, it gives and it takes, it enchants and it torments. Maybe to live between the sunshine and the hurricane, the bliss and the chaos is what writer-raconteur Eugene Walter meant when he described the Gulf Coast as "sweet lunacy."

It's how the bathwater-warm waves that wash boatloads of blue crab, flounder and shrimp onto the banks of Alabama's Mobile Bay in a jubilee come from the same basin as the storm surge that erases whole towns from Mississippi's edge like an Etch A Sketch. It's how kick after kick in the teeth Louisiana's residents rebuild taller and engineers construct levees stronger. It's how that 1966 Ford Thunderbird parked beside a concrete slab and an abandoned pool with an alligator floating in it sits next door to a beachfront mansion on Florida's Panhandle.

Within this landscape so rife with tragedy and exploitation, generations of people—French, West African, Cajun, Cuban, Vietnamese, Greek, Italian and more—have steeped abundant joy in their proverbial pot of traditions. Sugar-sanded king cakes on Twelfth Night, community oyster roasts at the docks, those newspaper-lined tables piled high with crawfish, even when times are low. The Gulf's one certainty: As sure as the sea and sky roil, the gumbo will boil. —The Editors

ESSENTIALS

*Trusted intel and travel info about iconic culture, geography
and entry points to the Gulf Coast's
traditions and landscape*

PLANNING

MICRO SKIFF
BOTE
Destin, FL
boteboard.com

....

FAT-TIRE BIKE
Neptune Cyclery
Tarpon Springs, FL
neptunecyclery.com

LANDMARK BRIDGES
LAKE PONTCHARTRAIN CAUSEWAY
New Orleans, LA
The world's longest bridge over
one body of water. Opened 1956.

....

SUNSHINE SKYWAY BRIDGE
St. Petersburg, FL
Four-mile cable-stayed bridge
across turquoise Tampa Bay.

MEDIA
RADIO SHOW
The Zest
Chefs, historians, farmers talk
Florida food on WUSF 89.7 FM.

....

MAGAZINE
64 Parishes
Nonprofit quarterly covers culture
in NOLA and low-lying Louisiana.

....

NEWSPAPER
Tampa Bay Times
Twelve-time Pulitzer winner.
Owned by revered Poynter Institute.

CLIMATE
The Gulf's seasons follow the
ebb and flow of people flocking
to its shores. Cane syrup–thick
humidity and tropical temps
spike in summer, and dew points
in the 90s are not uncommon
from Louisiana to Florida.
October [an underrated time to
visit] heralds crisper days ahead.
But, take note, hurricane season
[which starts in June] requires
a watchful eye and hardy spirit
until November. With cool but
comfortable days in winter, and
dreamy days in the 70s come
spring, snowbird residents
take to their roosts.

CALENDAR

JAN	30A Songwriters Festival
FEB	Mardi Gras
MAR	Gasparilla International Film Festival
APR	Louisiana Crawfish Boil Championships
MAY	Gulf Coast Wooden & Classic Boat Show
JUN	St. Pete Pride
JUL	Sarasota Lionfish Derby
AUG	Paddle at the Porch
SEP	Biloxi Seafood Festival
OCT	Cruisin' the Coast
NOV	Tampa Bay Times Festival of Reading
DEC	Christmas on the Water Boat Parade

GEOGRAPHY

Notable terrain formations and where to find them.

SAND DUNES
White sugar piles covered in sea oats, palmetto and beach morning glory provide first defense against hurricanes. *Grayton Beach State Park, FL*

MIDDENS
Man-made mountains of shells left behind by Indigenous people. The largest reaches 28 feet high. *Shell Mound on Cedar Key, FL*

BAYOUS
Placid, marshy rivulets and lakes home to migrating birds, fish, alligators, snakes and more. *Bayou Portage Coastal Preserve, MS*

ESTUARIES
Tidal streams where fresh water meets salty. Gulf home to a quarter of North America's estuaries. *Mobile Bay, AL*

SALT DOMES
More than 500 massive salt deposit pillars, thousands of feet tall, dot the entire Gulf. *Avery Island, LA*

WETLANDS
Waterlogged, flood-fed ecosystems. Disappearing landscape due to erosion and river diversion. *Port Eads, LA*

TRADITIONS

A heritage of farming, woodcraft and distilling.

Citrus
Oranges, grapefruits, lemons, satsumas and more thrive in the tropics. *The Citrus Place, Terra Ceia, FL*

Red Cypress
Long harvested for resilient qualities. Sinker logs from swamps particularly desired. *Bruner Lumber, Ponce De Leon, FL*

Architecture
Enduring styles include Creole cottages, shotguns, double-gallery porches, cracker wood frame and Spanish Colonial. *Preservation Resource Center, New Orleans, LA*

Wood Boats
From pirogues and canoes to sailboats and skiffs, wood boat building is a valued if vanishing craft. *Bill Holland, master boat builder, D'Iberville, MS*

Rum
Pre-Prohibition, the sugar cane–derived liquor was big business. And after, so was rum-running. Small distilleries are reviving the spirit. *Seven Three Distilling, New Orleans, LA*

FISHING DESTINATIONS

An approximate guide to recreational fishing spots and their noted catches.

GRAND ISLE, LA
Tarpon, speckled trout,
sheepshead

VENICE, LA
Redfish, yellowfin tuna,
red snapper

GULFPORT, MS
Permit, black drum,
amberjack

BILOXI BAY, MS
Vermilion snapper, cobia,
redfish

MOBILE BAY, AL
Speckled trout, tripletail,
flounder

DAUPHIN ISLAND, AL
Bluefish, cobia,
wahoo

DESTIN, FL
Black grouper, mahi-mahi,
blue marlin

CAPE SAN BLAS, FL
Pompano, triggerfish,
mullet

HOMOSASSA, FL
Snook, mangrove snapper,
scallops

FORT MYERS, FL
Redfish, gag grouper,
largemouth bass

CULTURAL INSTITUTIONS

WALTER ANDERSON MUSEUM OF ART
510 Washington Ave, Ocean Springs, MS

Dedicated to the South's "most elusive artist," naturalist and mystic.
Gallery of Anderson's work. Community center framed by his murals.

....

THE DALÍ
1 Dali Blvd, St. Petersburg, FL

Houses more than 2,400 works by supreme surrealist Salvador Dalí as well
as pieces related to his life and vision. Architected by Louvre chief of design.

....

CONTEMPORARY ARTS CENTER, NEW ORLEANS
900 Camp St, New Orleans, LA

Exhibition space for emerging and established Gulf South artists of all back-
grounds and disciplines, from painting and photography to dance and video.

SCENIC DRIVES
AND PUBLIC LANDS

Back-road journeys and natural sites across the Gulf.

HIGHWAY 90

The drive along Mississippi's Secret Coast runs a shell's toss to the water through historic towns with centuries-old oaks, Creole cottages and wraparound porch stunners. *Waveland to Pascagoula, MS*

....

ALABAMA COASTAL CONNECTION

U-shaped route rings around marshy Mobile Bay's fishing villages and makes a stop on Dauphin Island with white sand and day-glo stilt houses. Ride the ferry over to the eastern side. *Grand Bay to Daphne, AL*

....

BARATARIA PRESERVE

Only a half-hour from New Orleans, palmetto frond-lined boardwalk trail weaves through bird-serenaded swampland. Once provided refuge for escaping enslaved people. *Marrero, LA*

....

GREAT CALUSA BLUEWAY

Marked paddling trail connects 190 miles of water through the Estero Bay Aquatic Preserve, mangrove-forested Pine Island Sound and the Caloosahatchee River's tropical tributaries. Summer brings manatees into warm waters. *Sanibel Island to Fort Myers, FL*

....

ST. MARKS NATIONAL WILDLIFE REFUGE

A 68,000-acre Panhandle paradise for migrating and native birds in winter like roseate spoonbills, bald eagles and wood storks. Lighthouse from 1842. *St. Marks, FL*

....

WILLIAM J. RISH RECREATIONAL PARK

Named after a Florida state representative passionate about disability rights, the 100-acre beachfront park has 2 miles of ADA-compliant boardwalks and uninterrupted views. *Cape San Blas, FL*

....

BOCA GRANDE BIKE PATH

Peddle from the top of Gasparilla Island down a paved 6-mile bike lane into town and, farther, its namesake state park with a seashell-dusted beach and peacock-blue water. *Boca Grande, FL*

CULTURE

FILM

Beasts of the Southern Wild
Adaptation
Spring Breakers
Ulee's Gold
The Truman Show
Rosewood
Forrest Gump
The Order of Myths
Annihilation
Deepwater Horizon
Edward Scissorhands
Magic Mike

MUSIC

Bobby Charles
Bobby Charles

Jimmy Buffett
Living and Dying in 3/4 Time

Dave Bartholomew
In The Alley

John "Jab'o" Starks
"The Payback"

The Cannonball Adderley
Quintet
Somethin' Else

BOOKS

↦ *The Gulf: The Making of an American Sea* by Jack E. Davis: A Pulitzer Prize–earning tome traversing the Gulf from its geological creation to colonization to present-day disasters and preservation efforts.

↦ *The Rise and Decline of the Redneck Riviera* by Harvey H. Jackson III: Explores the development of a once-sleepy shoreline between Alabama and Florida into tourism giant and its economic, environmental consequences.

↦ *Like Trees, Walking* by Ravi Howard: A fictional rendering of a true story about a lynching in 1981 Mobile through the eyes of two brothers.

↦ *Salvage the Bones* by Jesmyn Ward: A National Book Award winner in which one family reckons with Hurricane Katrina and the wreckage it wreaks in their rural community, based on Ward's hometown, DeLisle, MS.

↦ *Journeys Through Paradise* by Gail Fishman: Recounts what naturalists Audubon, Muir and others experienced while exploring the Gulf.

↦ *The Awakening* by Kate Chopin: An early American feminist classic featuring clandestine lovers, infidelity, a toxic marriage, suicide and other dramas in 19th-century South Louisiana.

ISSUES

Disappearing Wetlands	Louisiana loses a football field's worth of wetlands every 100 minutes due to a tangle of factors like levee building, oil drilling, rising sea levels and the Mississippi River's diversion. Long-term solutions bring immediate costs to fishers and shrimpers. **EXPERT:** *Alyssa Dausman, Water Institute of the Gulf*
Hurricanes	The 2020 hurricane season was one of the Gulf's most active with eight land-falling storms. The tango between air pressure and La Niña is partly to blame, but rising water temperatures from climate change fuel the chances for more intense storms here in the future. **EXPERT:** *Eric Blake, National Hurricane Center*
Development	Land usage by the mega-industries of tourism and agriculture has fractured ecosystems, increased population density and made coastal communities more vulnerable to natural disasters. Fertilizer runoff causes toxic algae blooms and red tides. **EXPERT:** *Sabrina Cummings, Conservation Foundation of the Gulf Coast*
Wild Oysters	Apalachicola Bay once accounted for 90 percent of Florida's oyster harvest. After a 2012 drought left the area's fishery in shambles, the Florida Fish and Wildlife Conservation Commission unanimously voted in 2020 to stop oyster harvesting for five years so reefs could recover. Multigenerational seafood workers are out of work in the meantime. **EXPERT:** *Sandra Brooke, Florida State University*

STATISTICS

86 ....Average Gulf water temperature, in Fahrenheit, during August
177 ....Estimated number of wild chickens roaming Ybor City, FL
9 .... Where Gulf of Mexico ranks in largest bodies of water in the world
$3,360,000 ....Average price for Seaside, FL residential real estate
1/3............Asian population in Bayou La Batre, AL. Total residents: 2,500
200 ... Length of shrimp po' boy [in feet] served at Biloxi Seafood Festival

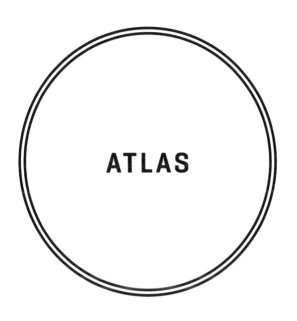

ATLAS

———

*A guide to the lands and places of the Gulf Coast,
including curated favorites, communities large and small,
and a ramble along Florida's shoreline*

BESTS

FOOD & DRINK

For seafood recommendations, see pages 72-73.

CUBAN BAKERY
La Segunda Bakery
2512 N 15th St
Ybor City, FL
Founded in 1915, run
by fourth-generation
family owners.
Old-style Cuban
bread, guava-cheese
turnovers.

....

NEW SOUTHERN
Southern National
360 Dauphin St
Mobile, AL
Chef Duane Nutter's
menu reflects the
cultural diversity of a
modern South.

....

GREEK
Hellas Restaurant
785 Dodecanese Blvd
Tarpon Springs, FL
Greek community
staple since 1970.
Saganaki and broiled
octopus.

MISSISSIPPI-JAPAN
Vestige
715 Washington Ave
Ocean Springs, MS
Husband-wife, Chef
Alex Perry and Kumi
Omori, give local
catches Japanese fla-
vor. Think blue crab
with koji bouillon.

....

WOOD-FIRED
Pêche
800 Magazine St
New Orleans, LA
Whole coal-cooked
fish, local oysters.
Raw bar seafood plat-
ter best deal in town.

....

IRISH PUB
Callaghan's
916 Charleston St
Mobile, AL
LA Burger [that's
lower Alabama] made
with Southern delicacy,
Conecuh sausage.

DOCKSIDE
Fisher's
17075 Marina Rd
Orange Beach, AL
Crab claws and black-
eyed pea hummus
downstairs. Grouper
gratin and crawfish
beignets upstairs.
Overlooks marina.

....

BÁNH MÌ
Le Bakery
280 Oak St
Biloxi, MS
Hoisin pork, daikon,
carrot, cucumber,
garlic mayo on house-
made French bread.

....

OYSTERS
Casamento's
4330 Magazine St
New Orleans, LA
Century-old, antique
tiled shoebox. Order a
dozen at the bar from
the shucker.

BARBECUE

The Shed
7501 Hwy 57
Ocean Springs, MS
Rambling roadhouse
with novel's worth of
signage. Choice ribs.
....

LOCAL CATCH

Owen's Fish Camp
516 Burns Ct
Sarasota, FL
Palmy courtyard
and tire swing. Get
the day's catch with
green-tomato salsa.
....

BURGER & BUSHWACKER

Pirates Cove
6664 CR 95
Elberta, AL
"Hole in the water"
going on 80 years.
Best reached by boat.
....

BREWERY

Cigar City Brewing
3924 W Spruce St
Tampa, FL
Craft beer pioneer
known for Jai Alai
and Hunahpu's Day.
....

NEIGHBORHOOD CAFE

Mockingbird Cafe
110 S 2nd St
Bay Saint Louis, MS
Early wake-up call
worth it for breakfast
biscuits on the porch.

ITALIAN

Mosca's
4137 US 90 W
Westwego, LA
Testament to Loui-
siana's overlooked
Italian heritage.
....

KING CAKE

**Dong Phuong
Bakeshop**
14207 Chef Menteur
New Orleans, LA
Cream cheese-frosted,
croissant-like wreaths
a once-a-year gift.
....

DEVIL CRAB

Brocato's
5021 E Columbus Dr
Tampa, FL
Crab croquettes a tra-
ditional cigar worker
treat. Never deviled.
....

DIVE

Old Point Bar
545 Patterson Rd
Algiers Point, LA
Sip an Abita amber
on the Mississippi
River levee.
....

THAI

Wat Tampa
5306 Palm River Rd
Tampa, FL
Mongkolratanaram
Buddhist temple
serves solid pad thai.

ALL-DAY CAFE

Bandit Coffee Co.
1662 Central Ave
St. Petersburg, FL
Hip roaster. Veggie
dishes, avant-garde
pastries, natty wine.
....

STEAKHOUSE

Bern's Steak House
1208 S Howard Ave
Tampa, FL
Leather-bound-
menu joint with in-
ternationally envied
wine selection.
....

BEACH BAR

Low Key Hideaway
12050 Hwy 24
Cedar Key, FL
Built from colored
bottles. Shrimp-
topped bloody mary.
....

FRIED SEAFOOD

Lorene's Fish House
927 22nd St S
St. Petersburg, FL
Fried whiting
sandwich with garlic
boiled peanuts.
....

ICE CREAM

Chill Bros.
1910 E 7th Ave
Ybor City, FL
Sibling-owned shop.
Flavors like Cream-
sicle, café con leche.

LODGING

OLD FLORIDA

The Gasparilla Inn
& Club

Boca Grande, FL
the-gasparilla-inn.com

Grand island resort
built in 1911. Still
has glamour that
attracted Old Holly-
wood here long ago.

....

ON THE BAY

Grand Hotel

Point Clear, AL
grand1847.com

Lakewood Golf Club
part of 550-acre live
oak-shaded campus.

....

HAUTE HISTORIC

Hotel Haya

Ybor City, FL
marriott.com

Details echo charm
of long-standing Cu-
ban neighborhood.

....

HOUSEBOAT

REEL Therapy

Venice, LA
vrbo.com

Upgraded floating cot-
tages at Louisiana's
southernmost point.

SUSTAINABLY MINDED

The Lodge at
Gulf State Park

Gulf Shores, AL
lodgeatgulfstatepark
.com

LEED-er in eco-
conscious hotel design.
Rooftop drink perch.

....

COASTAL CABIN

The Beatnik

Ocean Springs, MS
thehotelbeatnik.com

Ultramodern glass-
front cabins with
plunge pool, fire pit.

....

SMALL-TOWN SUITE

Pearl Hotel

Bay Saint Louis, MS
pearlbsl.com

Brand-new boutique
option on the Secret
Coast with a fresh-
thinking oyster bar.

....

CAJUN CONTEMPORARY

Tensas Tower on
the Teche

New Iberia, LA
airbnb.com

Futuristic lookout
and sculpture garden.

PINK PALACE

The Don CeSar

St. Petersburg, FL
doncesar.com

The "Grand Budapest"
on the beach with an
epic guest list from
F. Scott Fitzgerald to
Tom Petty.

....

WATERFRONT

Fenway Hotel

Dunedin, FL
fenwayhotel.com

Renovated Jazz Age
Spanish Colonial was
once a radio station.

....

VERANDA VIEW

The Gibson Inn

Apalachicola, FL
gibsoninn.com

A recently polished
Old Florida gem
from 1907. Wrap-
around balcony.

....

MICRO MOTEL

Camptel Resort

Cedar Key, FL
camptelglamping.com

Luxe tiny houses on
beach-lined isthmus
leading to island.

BOAT TOUR
Delta Discovery Tours
Buras, LA
deltadiscoverytours.com
Book the Birdsfoot Trip, an excursion past lighthouses and barrier islands to the Mississippi River's end.

....

DAY HIKE
Cathedral of Palms
Crawfordville, FL
A swampy grove vaulted in fronds hides a cerulean fish-filled spring.

....

SHUFFLEBOARD
St. Petersburg Shuffleboard Club
St. Petersburg, FL
stpeteshuffle.com
The country's oldest shuffleboard club. Standardized game's rules in the '20s.

....

SURFING
Pontcha Surf Club
@pontchasurf
Grand Isle guardians of Gulf surf culture. Lessons by appt.

SCUBA DIVING
Ginnie Springs
High Springs, FL
ginniespringsoutdoors.com
Plunge into turquoise water and swim toward the Ginnie Ballroom cavern. Gear rental available.

....

AQUARIUM
Dauphin Island Sea Lab
Dauphin Island, AL
disl.edu
Talk to experts on the Living Marsh Boardwalk tour.

....

BOTANICAL GARDEN
Bellingrath
Theodore, AL
bellingrath.org
Main attraction: azaleas aflame in flamingo pink, fruit punch and tangerine.

....

SWIMMING HOLE
Cold Hole
Magnolia Springs, AL
Take a tube to this oak- and cypress-canopied river refuge.

SCALLOPING
Happy Ours
Port St. Joe, FL
happyourskayak.com
Late-summer snorkeling hunts in secluded St. Joseph Bay. Bring a cooler.

....

FLATS FISHING
Oklahoma Flat
Homosassa, FL
Crystal water with rock bottom gives clear view of fish. Home to record tarpon catches.

....

PADDLE
Wacissa & Aucilla Rivers
Jefferson County, FL
Drop in at Wacissa public boat ramp. Glide over ice-blue water into a lush Shangri-La.

....

CHICKEN SPOTTING
Ybor Chickens Society
Ybor City, FL
yborchickens.org
Tracker for neighborhood's famous fowl.

SHOPS

BOUTIQUE
Joseph's Cottage
403 Reid Ave
Port St. Joe, FL
Melissa Farrell has
a keen eye for Old
Florida ephemera.
Linen kaftans, oyster
dishes, dried starfish.

....

GOURMET MARKET
Provision
100 N Section St
Fairhope, AL
Bottle shop's ban-
quette lounge so entic-
ing you may open that
pét-nat early.

....

MARINE SUPPLY
Whidden's Marina
190 First St E
Boca Grande, FL
A 1926 relic [once a
dance hall] with bait,
gas, "cold beer and
great conversation."

....

ZERO WASTE
Sans Market
1037 Central Ave
St. Petersburg, FL
Metal straws, soap re-
fills, bamboo brushes.

OUTFITTER
Bill Jackson's Shop
for Adventure
9501 US 19 N
Pinellas Park, FL
Founded in 1946 by
early adopter of rec-
reational scuba. Try
out gear at store's
lake, carpeted ski
slope, indoor pool.

....

FARM STAND
Forbes Road Produce
Exit 17 off Rt 4
Plant City, FL
Plant City known for
its sweet strawberries.

....

MARDI GRAS SUPPLY
Toomey's
755-A McRae Ave
Mobile, AL
A 70,000-sq-ft trove
of beads, parasols,
float throws, etc.

....

VINTAGE
La France
1612 E 7th Ave
Ybor City, FL
Everything to look
like an extra in 1967's
Clambake.

ORCHIDS
Palmer Orchids
11700 Taylor Dr
Bradenton, FL
Longtime pur-
veyor's greenhouses
brim with Tech-
nicolor blooms.

....

ANTIQUES
Charles Phillips
4505 Laurendine Rd
Theodore, AL
Rural reverie for
old-house lovers.
Transom doors, shut-
ters, cast-iron gates.

....

ALL-IN-ONE
Oxford Exchange
420 W Kennedy Blvd
Tampa, FL
Bookstore, home
goods, cafe, clubhouse.

....

BOOKSTORES
Sundog Books
Seaside, FL
Tombolo Books
St. Petersburg, FL
Pass Christian Books
Pass Christian, MS
Gene's Books
Sanibel, FL

ARTS & CRAFT

SKIFFS
Caribiana
Orange Beach, AL
caribiana.com
Custom builder
of flat-bottomed,
crescent-shaped
boats. Teak touches
throughout.

....

PHOTOGRAPHY
Florida Museum of
Photographic Arts
Tampa, FL
fmopa.org
Inside the Cube build-
ing. Work by Lange,
Niccolini, Uzzle.

....

GAS LANTERNS
Bevolo
New Orleans, LA
bevolo.com
Gold standard for
open-flame copper
lanterns.

....

QUILTS
Ground Zero Museum
Waveland, MS
*wavelandground
zero.com*
Handiwork focused
on Hurricane Katrina.

FLY TYING
239 Flies
Bonita Springs, FL
239flies.com
Feathers, deer belly
hair, flash, hooks
and the know-how to
tie it all together.

....

ART MUSEUM
The Ringling
Sarasota, FL
ringling.org
Circus founder's Ve-
netian Gothic home,
plus 21 galleries,
gardened grounds.

....

MOVIE PALACE
Tampa Theatre
Tampa, FL
tampatheatre.org
Ornate example of
Atmospheric Theatre.
Shows first-run indies.

....

CERAMICS
Ohr-O'Keefe
Museum of Art
Biloxi, MS
georgeohr.org
Frank Gehry–
designed building for
master potter's work.

RESIDENCY
Rauschenberg
Residency on Captiva
Captiva, FL
*rauschenberg
foundation.org*
Live, work in the
postmodernist
painter's Fish House.

....

PUBLIC ART
Milagros Collective
Louisiana/Florida
@milagrosyall
Creates colorful,
provocative
installations out of
overlooked spaces.

....

ARCHITECTURE
Cocoon House
Sarasota, FL
saf-srq.org
Peak midcentury de-
sign cantilevered on
Siesta Key lagoon.

....

MUSICAL PLAYGROUND
Music Box Village
New Orleans, LA
musicboxvillage.com
Interactive instru-
mental treehouses at
Bywater's edge.

EVENTS

BOOKS & AUTHORS

Tampa Bay Times Festival of Reading

Tampa, FL
tampabay.com

Readings by bestselling and local authors. Free to the public.

....

CAR SHOW

Cruisin' the Coast

Mississippi
cruisinthecoast.com

More than 8,000 classic cars on display along Highway 90.

....

MUSIC FESTIVAL

T-Bois Blues Festival

Larose, LA
tboisblues.com

Camp on an alligator farm for swamp rock, blues, Cajun bands and bonfires.

....

ARTS & CRAFTS

Peter Anderson Festival

Ocean Springs, MS
@peterandersonfestival

Hundreds of artists, fine and folk, set up under downtown oaks.

SEAFOOD FESTIVALS

Florida Seafood Festival

Apalachicola, FL
floridaseafoodfestival.com

Oyster shucking contest, blue crab races and a blessing of the fleet in Oyster Bay.

....

Biloxi Seafood Festival

Biloxi, MS
biloxi.org

Heated gumbo championship and 200-foot po'boy.

....

PRIDE

St. Pete Pride

St. Petersburg, FL
stpetepride.org

Florida's largest Pride parade emblematic of city.

....

BOAT PARADE

Manatee River Holiday Boat Parade

Palmetto, FL
holidayboatparade.org

Yachts, skiffs and sailboats decked out in Christmas lights.

BIRDING

Florida Birding & Nature Festival

Brandon, FL
floridabirdingand
naturefestival.org

Four-day gathering of naturalists mixes seminars, field trips.

....

REGATTA

Juana Good Time

Navarre Beach, FL
juanaspagodas.com

Professional but laid-back competition. Live music. Handmade trophies.

....

DINNER SERIES

Southern Grace

Orange Beach, AL
fishersobm.com

Acclaimed chefs collab for one-time only menus at Fisher's.

....

STEP COMPETITION

Stompfest

Pensacola, FL
stompfest850.com

HBCU stepping event with celeb DJs like Mannie Fresh.

EXPERTS

CULTURE
New Orleans Center
for the Gulf South
@NOCGS
Tulane University's
multifaceted insti-
tute for the study of
Gulf Coast culture.

....

BLACK HISTORY
Kern Jackson
*University of South
Alabama*
Helping efforts to
build museum in
Mobile's Africatown
for *Clotilda* slave ship.

....

ARBORNAUT
Meg Lowman
TREE Foundation
Nicknamed "Canopy
Meg" and the real-
life Lorax. Global
forest conservation
authority.

....

TUPELO HONEY
Ben Lanier
lltupelohoney.com
Third-generation
beekeeper tends
hives of Panhandle's
rare honey.

NATURE PHOTOGRAPHY
Carlton Ward
@carltonward
Conservation pho-
tographer captures
Florida wildlife.
Started "Path of the
Panther" project.

....

AIR MANEUVERS
Lt. Julius Bratton
U.S. Navy Blue Angels
Blue Angel #7
narrates the
Pensacola-based
flight crew's air show
with precise timing.

....

BAYKEEPER
Casi Callaway
Mobile Baykeeper
Mobile native
protected "America's
Amazon" for 23
years.

....

METEOROLOGIST
Margaret Orr
WDSU News
Redheaded saint of
hurricane season in
southeast Louisiana.
On air at WDSU
since 1979.

VIETNAMESE ADVOCACY
Daniel Le
Boat People SOS
Provides health and
education resources
for fishing commu-
nities in Biloxi and
Bayou La Batre.

....

CLIMATE CHANGE
Nathaniel Rich
nathanielrich.com
NOLA-based author
of *Losing Earth* stud-
ies existential threats
to Gulf Coast's eco-
systems and people.

....

BOTTARGA
Seth & Mic Cripe
Cortez Conservas
Anna Maria Island
brothers' cured
mullet roe imparts
instant umami.

....

OYSTER FARMING
Brent & Rosa Zirlott
Murder Point Oysters
Zirlott family's
small, buttery
oysters have a big
chef cult following.
Grown on AL coast.

CITIES & TOWNS

The coast is flocked with cosmopolitan ports, working fishing villages and provincial outposts. Here, twelve communities that tell its full story.

AVERY ISLAND & NEW IBERIA, LA

In 1868, Edmund McIlhenny planted his first crop of peppers. He named the resulting hot sauce TABASCO, an Indigenous Mexican word believed to mean "place where the soil is humid." To this day, the Tabasco factory, still run by his descendants, sits atop Avery Island, a precarious pillar of salt in Louisiana's southern marshes. Its verdant, wild acreage inspired the name for JUNGLE GARDENS, the botanical preserve started by McIlhenny's son Ned, who planted some of the 450 camellia specimens that scatter the ground with petals each winter. In neighboring New Iberia, BON CREOLE LUNCH COUNTER serves its gumbo Acadiana-style with a scoop of potato salad in the middle, and LEGNON'S BOUCHERIE has plenty of ways to take a bit of the bayou back with you, from boudin sausage to cracklins.

HISTORY STOP	POPULATION: 29,751
Rip Van Winkle Gardens	COFFEE: Cafe Jefferson
A silent movie star's Steamboat Gothic mansion	BEST DAY OF THE YEAR: World Championship Gumbo Cookoff, October

NEW ORLEANS, LA

Whiling away the day with a cocktail in a French Quarter courtyard, it's easy to forget there's a whole world of water behind the 192 miles of levee walls that keep New Orleans dry. But the city's connection to the Gulf is ever-present, from Donald Link's PÊCHE, where whole redfish, flounder and snapper cook over a wood-fired grill, to Bywater green space CRESCENT PARK, where boats glide in from open water up the Mississippi River. Ride across the river yourself on the Algiers Point ferry to CONGREGATION COFFEE, a corner cafe nestled in a neighborhood of Creole cottages. A bit farther past the West Bank, pick oranges, Meyer lemons and satsumas in the shadow of container ships at ISABELLE'S ORANGE ORCHARD, a riverside grove lovingly tended by French transplant and tour guide Isabelle Cossart.

PARK STOP	POPULATION: 388,424
The Fly	COFFEE: Hey Cafe! at Tipitina's
Locals love to relax at Audubon Park's river-facing side	BEST DAY OF THE YEAR: Crawfish season in full swing, March

BAY SAINT LOUIS, MS

Just a hop over from the Crescent City, Bay Saint Louis has long been a safe harbor for New Orleanians looking to stretch out. This small town may lack the drama of sand dunes, but with the beach just a saunter away, it can easily lure you in. As can the sense of community. Locals and vacationers alike sit on the three-sided gallery porch, circa 1868, of MOCKINGBIRD CAFE with breakfast biscuit sandwiches and gather at ST. ROSE DE LIMA, a historically Black Catholic church [with a fascinating cemetery] for Lent season fish fries. Two new-ish additions form BSL's best dinner-and-a-show: THORNY OYSTER's raw bar for grouper ceviche and 100 MEN HALL D.B.A., an important venue on the Chitlin' Circuit recently revived for a new generation of Southern musicians.

BEACH STOP	POPULATION: 15,066
Ship Island	COFFEE: Mockingbird Cafe
Barrier island with secluded shores reachable by ferry	BEST DAY OF THE YEAR: Twelfth Night, January

OCEAN SPRINGS, MS

When Annette McConnell Anderson was an art student in the 1890s, her professor said that for Southern artists to succeed, they would have to stop focusing on Northern scenery and capture the beauty around them. She, in turn, instilled that ethos in her sons, who became artists too in Ocean Springs. In 1928, Peter Anderson founded SHEARWATER POTTERY, now operated by his son, Jim, and grandson, Peter Wade. The showroom's pottery forms, made from Gulf-sourced clay, glazed in greens and blues, echo the colors in the work by Peter's brother, Walter, on display at the WALTER ANDERSON MUSEUM OF ART. Many of his mystical, Gauguin-esque watercolors of pelicans, turtles and fish were inspired by HORN ISLAND, now a sanctioned wilderness area. It's a more than worthwhile endeavor to charter a boat out to this Eden of Southern species, from terrapins to ghost crabs.

DINNER STOP	POPULATION: 17,729
Vestige	COFFEE: Bright-Eyed Brew Co.
Local ingredients prepared with Japanese techniques	BEST DAY OF THE YEAR: Cruisin' the Coast, October

MOBILE, AL

Alabama's port city, pronounced "Mo-BEEL," rhymes with "genteel," an apt adjective to describe its oak-lined avenues and graceful Creole architecture. This city also has a raucous spirit, though, especially at Mardi Gras, and, boy, its citizens won't let you forget they celebrated it first. Modern-day Mobile's downtown has more happening under its cast-iron balconies than expected, notably the nationally recognized restaurant SOUTHERN NATIONAL and craft cocktail bar THE HABERDASHER. But downtown isn't where you'll find one of the South's best small venues. That would be in the sleepy Washington Square neighborhood, where John "J.T." Thompson, owner of canteen CALLAGHAN'S IRISH SOCIAL CLUB, brings in musicians before they hit the big time [and sometimes ones who already have].

SHOP STOP	POPULATION: 190,432
The Cheese Cottage	COFFEE: Nova Espresso
Bottle shop with specialty wedges	BEST DAY OF THE YEAR: St. Patrick's Day, March

GULF SHORES & ORANGE BEACH, AL

What a glass of chardonnay is to Napa a bushwacker—the frozen concoction of ice cream, chocolate, coffee and dark rum—is to Alabama's coast. Lest the area's official beverage allow you to write off these twin beach towns as unsophisticated, ascend to FISHER'S upstairs dining room, perched over Orange Beach Marina, for chef Bill Briand's blue crab-stuffed flounder or Bon Secour oysters in garlic-leek butter. Another proof point: THE LODGE AT GULF STATE PARK holds LEED platinum certification for how it has seamlessly integrated itself into the refuge's 6,500 acres, home to nesting sea turtles in summer. Of course, if you're this close to the state line, you might as well step into the belly of the beast at the infamously rowdy roadhouse FLORA-BAMA, which hosts the annual Interstate Mullet Toss, a competition of throwing dead fish across the sand—just as bizarre as it sounds.

LUNCH STOP	POPULATION: 18,286
Anchor Bar & Grill	COFFEE: Foam Coffee
Burgers and bushwackers on marooned ship's deck	BEST DAY OF THE YEAR: Hangout Music Festival, March

GRAYTON BEACH, FL

Compared with the rest of Highway 30A's planned communities, with their covenants and codes, Grayton Beach remains a lovable misfit. Exhibit A: the town's unofficial slogan, "Nice dogs, strange people." Founded in 1890, this hippie-ish hamlet has more tin-roofed cracker cottages and ancient magnolias than leisure palaces and professional landscaping. Beloved beach bar legend THE RED BAR has been rebuilt in such exact detail you wouldn't know it burned down in 2019. [Its resident jazz band grooves good as ever.] James Beard Award–nominated baker Debbie Swenerton crafts artisan loaves and pastries at BLACK BEAR BREAD CO. Munch on a bear claw and sip a Stumptown iced coffee on the drive into GRAYTON BEACH STATE PARK, a 2,000-acre preserve with placid dune lakes for stand-up paddleboarding and a sandy trail through a thicket of twisted scrub oaks that yields to azure waves.

FISHING STOP	POPULATION: 17,213
Captain Phil's Charters	COFFEE: Hibiscus Coffee & Guesthouse
Spikes the day's catch on the side of the boat	BEST DAY OF THE YEAR: 30A Songwriters Festival, January

PENSACOLA, FL

Pensacola has a history as a shared city. The Spanish, French and British all arrived here, and today it feels as much a part of Florida as it does Alabama. Take it slow and wake up at the COFFEE CUP RESTAURANT before slipping into the woods at NAVAL LIVE OAKS NATURE PRESERVE overlooking Pensacola Bay. Back across the bridge, a walking tour in the Seville Historic District or an afternoon excursion to FORT PICKENS provides a quick study in global influences: architectural, political and military. GEORGE BISTRO + BAR has prettied-up deviled eggs and a veggie plate for a proper Southern sit-down, but you could also take a basket of picnic provisions from THE FARM to a spot high up in the dunes.

WILDLIFE STOP	POPULATION: 53,651
Gulf Islands National Seashore	COFFEE: Bodacious Bookstore & Café
Search out a freshwater pond in the dunes	BEST DAY OF THE YEAR: Foo Foo Festival, November

TAMPA, FL

The third wheel to Orlando and Miami [although the Super Bowl–winning Buccaneers may be changing that], Tampa is content to play the role of unassuming beauty. Set out with YBOR CITY HISTORIC WALKING TOURS to learn how Cuban Americans built Cigar City, then experience another thriving Ybor tradition: real-deal Cuban sandwiches piled high with mojo-marinated pork at LA SEGUNDA BAKERY. Downtown, wander into the TAMPA MUSEUM OF ART, which glows along the Hillsborough River thanks to Leo Villareal's LED installation *Sky [Tampa]*. For more evidence of Tampa's underrated arts scene, see Seminole Heights' TEMPUS PROJECTS, which curates work by contemporary Floridian artists like Kalup Linzy. Just a short drive northward, MERMAID TAVERN has wild catfish on the smoker and bartenders who know just the right bottle of natty white to pair with it.

SKATE STOP	POPULATION: 404,636
Bro Bowl	COFFEE: King State
Florida's first public skate park	BEST DAY OF THE YEAR: Gasparilla Pirate Festival, January

ST. PETERSBURG, FL

St. Petersburg's Old Florida charm persists even with a recent polishing. Explore its natural side at FORT DESOTO's beaches and coastal hammocks on foot or stalk its edges in a kayak. For lunch, go downtown and order a pollo frita sandwich and mango smoothie at BODEGA followed by an easy-going day drink with a Postcard pilsner at GREEN BENCH BREWING. If an afternoon squall looms on the horizon, take a beat and carve through HASLAM'S BOOK STORE, the state's oldest and largest independent bookseller, where Jack Kerouac's ghost sometimes appears. By the time the light softens, meander the bayfront parks or drive south to BOYD HILL NATURE PRESERVE. For dinner and drinks, hit a high-low combo on Central Avenue at tropical-tilting WILD CHILD before wood-paneled dive EMERALD BAR.

GARDEN STOP	POPULATION: 271,842
Sunken Gardens	COFFEE: Bandit
Ancient sinkhole turned botanical garden known for flamingos	BEST DAY OF THE YEAR: Tampa Bay Times Festival of Reading, November

ROAD TRIP

*For a coastal odyssey of Florida landscapes, flavors, culture and history,
start this ramble in the Panhandle and wander southward.*

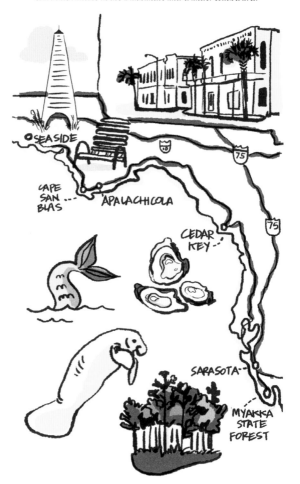

SEASIDE

CAPE
SAN
BLAS

APALACHICOLA

75

75

CEDAR
KEY

SARASOTA

MYAKKA
STATE
FOREST

PANHANDLE PROMENADE

A mix of shoreline outposts—company town to master-planned community—is standing proof of Florida's history of opportunism and optimism.

Director Peter Weir had almost given up on a location for *The Truman Show* and settled for a soundstage in Los Angeles when his wife found the "master-planned" community of Seaside on Florida's now-famed Highway 30A. Although its cheerful Chiclet-like cottages and cute post office provided the ideal backdrop for the manufactured and closely surveilled life of perfection in the movie, the real Seaside isn't exactly Stepford. Pop into decidedly unconventional SUNDOG BOOKS and CENTRAL SQUARE RECORDS, perched over the same beachside town square [more like a semicircle] where Seaside Farmers Market shoppers pick up locally grown oranges and tupelo honey. The community also hosts the annual 30A SONGWRITERS FESTIVAL [Emmylou Harris, John Prine, Jason Isbell all alumni] and the Longleaf Writers Conference. Drive past 30A's high-dollar vacation villas [there's a reason this stretch is called the Hamptons of the South] and a more modest, midcentury scene comes into view at Laguna Beach, where you can still eat a reasonably priced diner-style burger at the THOMAS DONUT AND SNACK SHACK and enjoy an uninterrupted view of the water. At nearby ST. ANDREWS STATE PARK, the egalitarian access belies its uncrowded beach, a 10-out-of-10 stunner with Coke bottle–green waves and rock jetties. Take the road less traveled, away from Panama City Beach's stretch of high-rises and souvenir shops, into St. Andrews, a historic downtown in the midst of a revival. Sit on the patio of new addition, HISTORY CLASS BREWING COMPANY, and sip a pint of Pretty Bayou, then take a stroll past the Martin Theatre, an art deco gem, to the corner of 9th Street and Calhoun Avenue to marvel at the front yard tropicalia of Mike and Cindi Cole, owners of the Snooty Gardener. An hour down the highway past Mexico Beach [brake for Killer Seafood's trailer if it's open], Port St. Joe was, in 1837, once the largest outpost in the Florida territory. After yellow fever and a hurricane very nearly wiped it off the map, the settlement was reimagined by 20th-century entrepreneurs as a company town around a paper mill. The mill closed in 1999, and today's Port St. Joe is sleepier, but it's no less charming—the kind of place to rent a cottage on short notice, settle into the porch swing and finally read the novel that's been languishing on your nightstand. When you venture into downtown, stop in at JOSEPH'S COTTAGE, a boutique owned by Melissa Farrell, who—together with Christina McDermott and Emily Raffield—authored *Saints of Old Florida*, a coveted coffee table book that captures the hidden romance and history of this part of the Panhandle.

DAY 2

THE FORGOTTEN COAST

Also known as the Emerald Coast, this serene stretch has been left mostly alone by property hawks and development prospectors.

CAPE SAN BLAS On a map, it looks like a glorified sandbar, but this sliver might be one of the Gulf's best-kept secrets. A row of stilt houses lines 30E., the one road on this peaceful peninsula where even during peak season you'll find just a few souls strolling abreast the waves. On the fittingly named STUMP HOLE BEACH, ancient cypress stumps stand suspended over the sand by exposed roots once submerged in the water. A more recent landmark worth the mile-ish hike down the beach: the DONNA KAY, a shrimping boat run aground in 2018 in the surge before Hurricane Michael. How it got here? Theories abound, from a sleepy captain to insurance fraud.

....

APALACHICOLA A recent short-term ban on harvesting wild oysters in its estuary has been a hard hit for this salty yet seductive town, but thanks to oyster farms and harvests from nearby counties, there are still plenty of half-shell opportunities, namely HOLE IN THE WALL with its bantering staff, THE STATION RAW BAR and on the wraparound veranda of THE GIBSON INN, a renovated stunner built in 1907. On Commerce Street, pop in at BECASA, where Emily Raffield [yes, from *Saints of Old Florida*] sells breezy linen pieces she also happens to design. Just a block farther, pull up at the oversize cypress benches at OYSTER CITY BREWING with a Mangrove pale ale. You'll quickly make some new friends, maybe even fishing buddies.

....

ST. VINCENT ISLAND Home to red wolves, nests of least tern and tufts of amethyst-colored Gulf Coast lupine, this barrier island wildlife refuge is accessible only by boat. Take the shuttle ferry over, or experience its natural wonders just by standing at the pier near INDIAN PASS CAMPGROUND at the end of 30B, where pods of bottlenose dolphins put on their own show.

....

CRAWFORDVILLE An untouched primordial paradise for migrating and native birds in winter, ST. MARKS NATIONAL WILDLIFE REFUGE spans 68,000 acres with plenty of lookout towers for spotting roseate spoonbills, bald eagles, even wood storks. The 19th-century lighthouse has survived multiple hurricanes and the Civil War. As you drive out of the refuge, head to Ouzts' Too Oyster Bar and Grill for smoked mullet and a dozen on a cafeteria tray, best eaten in the courtyard under banana trees.

THE BIG BEND

This is the part of Florida no one told you about:
the unconsidered coast. More commonly known as the
Nature Coast, it is far away, pristine and fierce.

BY FOOT

The ECONFINA RIVER draws a series of arcs through old-growth forests
until it spills into the Gulf. Follow CR 14 until it ends and continue
west by foot to see coastal Florida as it was centuries ago. There the
impossibly beautiful BLUE TRAIL meanders through 49 hammock
islands and past 11 cerulean springs.

BY PADDLE

Stick to U.S. 98, then head south on Highway 51 to the foot of STEINHATCHEE
FALLS. From there, the Adventure Outpost's naturalists will carry you
down one of Florida's lesser-known rivers. Look for greenfly orchids in
the fall and butterfly orchids in late spring.

BY BOAT

If it's tenable, consider pooling your funds to hire a guide with a skiff,
whether it's to stalk tarpon, harvest scallops or see the seemingly endless nexus of serpentine creeks and spring-fed rivers as they meet the
Gulf. Give Captain Lacey Kelly with FLORIDA OUTDOOR EXPERIENCE a
shout and book one of her flats fishing excursions to catch some snook.

SECRET SPRINGS

For centuries, Florida's natural springs have
enticed weary travelers yearning for good health
and relaxation.

Florida is home to more large-size natural springs than any other state, and the healing, sapphire-blue allure of those along the Gulf's edge has drawn Old World explorers and old Hollywood celebrities alike. Evade the syrupy humidity with a 90-minute float in RAINBOW SPRINGS, or hop aboard a covered pontoon ride through CRYSTAL RIVER PRESERVE STATE PARK's estuary. Citrus County is the only place where it's legal to swim with manatees in their natural habitat; sanctioned snorkeling tours at Crystal River offer a chance to float [with reverence] among the calm, curious creatures. Back on dry land, head south on U.S. 19 to the first-magnitude spring at HOMOSASSA SPRINGS WILDLIFE STATE PARK and its exotic wildlife, which includes flamingos and Lucifer, the oldest hippopotamus in captivity. Farther south, at WEEKI WACHEE SPRINGS STATE PARK, make time to see one of the famed mermaid shows. Fish-tailed beauties have been dancing underwater since 1947, gulping air through long hoses in between graceful flips and kicks.

<table>
<tr><td>DAY
5</td><td>

OLD FLORIDA

Journey through the wild and civil sides of Sarasota, where its mangrove forests and unswept beaches meet city vestiges, both quaint and grand.
</td></tr>
</table>

The Myakka River name remains a mystery. Some believe it comes from the Timucua word for large ["*mayaca*"], while others claim the name is related to the Mayaimi tribe. To get a sense of its myth and lore for yourself—and a feel for the wildness and complexity of this area just east of Sarasota—start at MYAKKA RIVER STATE PARK. From the main gate, head north until you reach Clay Gully, a black ribbon of water hemmed in by oaks and sabal palms. Osprey and anhinga soar above while alligators sunbathe in the mud below. A mile in, the landscape rises into an oak hammock bordering Florida's most biologically diverse landscape, dry prairie. Keep an eye out for more raptors, namely the crested caracara, but also bald eagles, hawks and scrub jays. As you slip back into the pine scrub, look for wild blueberries or an ancient lemon tree. Back in the car, follow U.S. 75 south to River Road, where a narrow path through the trees spits you out at SNOOK HAVEN, a fish camp along an oxbow of the Myakka that was once used for smuggling alcohol and distilling moonshine. After emerging from the wilds, wander into the heart of Sarasota and stroll the graceful grounds of MARIE SELBY BOTANICAL GARDENS, a corner of town along Hudson Bayou and Sarasota Bay lush with tropical trees, orchids and native plants. Up the bay, THE JOHN AND MABLE RINGLING MUSEUM OF ART, founded by the circus mogul and his wife in 1927, comprises 21 galleries and Ca' d'Zan, their splendid Venetian Gothic residence. From there, follow the sun west to Lido Key and sneak around the bend to an undeveloped beach that feels miles away, yet still tethered to the city. Back in town, grab drinks and oysters at OWENS FISH CAMP in its twinkle-lit backyard shaded by a giant banyan tree as a string band picks away. Lastly, a mandatory nightcap at Sarasota's dearest dive, MEMORIES LOUNGE. Say hi to the bar's resident nonagenarian, Philip Hall [known to sing "Hava Nagila" on Fridays], and ask him to tell you a joke.

> *A string of less famous but still pretty keys borders Sarasota. On Longboat, sit a spell at all-day cafe Whitney's. At Bird Key's public park, bring a pole, paddleboard or picnic. Or order up a dozen on the half shell at Siesta Key Oyster Bar.*

MORE THAN 30 ENTRIES ⮞

ALMANAC

*A deep dive into the cultural heritage of
the Gulf Coast through news clippings, timelines,
writings and other historical hearsay*

TUPELO HONEY

Liquid gold, genuine tupelo honey comes from a small sliver of Florida's
Panhandle and is harvested during an even tinier time frame.
With a chartreuse cast and a buttery, Creamsicle-like taste, the honey
is increasingly rare and expensive [commanding $31 per pound]
as tupelo trees endure increasing hurricanes and climate change.
Early accounts of the industry follow.

"Throughout the Apalachicola valley, as they term it, one can kick the
hound dogs around, steal a flivver for a joy ride or spank the neighbor's
children and get away with it, but if one lonesome, solitary, wandering bee
is molested there is more trouble on the horizon in 10 seconds than China
and Nicaragua could produce in six months."
—*The Palm Beach Post*, March 1, 1927

"For fifty years, the tupelo honey producers of Calhoun, Liberty and
Franklin counties have worked their apiaries until a honeyed aristocracy
has been built up. The apiaries are cherished by families much as
heirlooms, while serving as a means of livelihood to the other."
—*The Miami News*, November 24, 1922

"Tupelo honey does not crystalize. It is now being sought as a center for
golf balls, taking the place of rubber and other substances once used. One
Apalachicola firm producing tupelo honey last year sold a solid car load of
the product to a golf ball manufacturer."
—*Tallahassee Democrat*, November 5, 1935

"The tupelo kingdom is a limited one, reaching from 10 miles north
of Blountstown along the banks of the Apalachicola River, to a point
five miles north of Apalachicola. There is no area to fall back on. For
tupelo honey, this is the spot, honey men say."
—*The Tampa Tribune*, February 19, 1950

Panhandle honey producer Ben Lanier consulted on the film
ULEE'S GOLD, *which starred Peter Fonda as a widowed beekeeper.*
The performance earned Fonda an Oscar nomination.

JOHN JAMES AUDUBON

Famed illustrator John James Audubon's iconic elephant-size folio
The Birds of America was partially inspired by the ornithologist's
adventures along the Gulf Coast. He completed at least 167 of the book's 435
drawings while living in Louisiana and even claimed to have been born on
a Mandeville plantation [Audubon was born in what is now Haiti to his
father's mistress]. Below, a selection of Gulf birds included in the survey.

BROWN PELICAN, *Plate 251*

LOUISIANA HERON, *Plate 217*

FISH CROW, *Plate 146*

WHOOPING CRANE, *Plate 226*

WHITE HERON, *Plate 386*

ROSEATE SPOONBILL, *Plate 321*

AMERICAN COOT, *Plate 239*

BLACK-HEADED GULL, *Plate 314*

FISH HAWK (OSPREY), *Plate 81*

MARSH TERN, *Plate 410*

WHITE IBIS, *Plate 222*

BARTRAM SANDPIPER, *Plate 303*

> *Naturalist and "Father of the National Parks" John Muir also spent time*
> *on the Gulf with a particularly memorable stint in then-busy Cedar Key.*
> *Muir collapsed with a fever, possibly malaria, while in search of lemons in*
> *town. After three months, he recovered and hopped a schooner for Cuba.*

SHELL MOUNDS

Considered the first shell collectors, Florida's Indigenous Calusa people were once the most powerful group along the coast of Southwest Florida. They piled millions of seashells, oyster shells and bones into mounds that were wide enough to build structures on top and tall enough to tower above floods. Tribes also used the mounds as a place for rituals and burying the dead, while waterways surrounding the structures proved useful for travel and trading. The Calusa also used shells in many other aspects of life, in tools, weapons, decorative artwork and jewelry. Because of this, they have been called "the shell people," "mound people" and "pile dwellers." Several small shell mound islands still exist in the waters off Florida's west coast. Two of note: the one at Sanibel's J.N. "Ding" Darling Wildlife Refuge and a 20-foot-high prehistoric mound at the "A Window to the Past" exhibit in Historic Spanish Point in Sarasota County.

ALLIGATORS

"ALLIGATORS NO GOOD AS PETS, KEEPER SAYS"
It isn't safe to wrestle them either
Tampa Bay Tribune, August 11, 1929

Persons desiring a live alligator for a household pet are advised by W.L. Collins, owner of an alligator farm at Sulphur Springs, not to steal it, no matter how small. It embarrasses the alligator as well as the person caught with the reptile in his pocket, he said. Few visitors attempt to swipe a 'gator from the farm, and still fewer escape with their "swag." Collins describes the attempt of a man who tried to steal a couple of 'gators as a lark. "He put two in his pocket and stuffed his handkerchief on top of them so they couldn't get out. ...He denied he had any alligators on him, and sure did turn red when I pulled both of them out of his pocket."

EARLY COLONIZERS AND EXPLORERS

JUAN PONCE DE LEÓN [*apprx. 1460–1521*]
Spanish conquistador led his own expedition in 1513 to the coast to look for the "fountain of youth." He gave the land before him the name "Florida," meaning flowery, which seemed fitting for the territory's verdant landscape.

....

ALONSO ÁLVAREZ DE PINEDA [1494–1520]
Spanish cartographer sailed around the Gulf of Mexico—what he called "Amichel"—and drew the first European map of the present-day coast. He also proved Florida was a peninsula and that there was no direct sea passage to Asia.

....

HENRI DE TONTI [*apprx. 1649–1704*]
Born in Sicily, raised in France, military officer journeyed down the Mississippi River in 1682, reached its mouth and claimed the surrounding territory for Louis the Great. He was nicknamed "Iron Hand" due to the prosthetic appendage he donned, always covered with a glove.

....

JEAN-BAPTISTE LE MOYNE DE BIENVILLE [1680–1767]
French-Canadian explorer served as four-term governor of French Louisiana, founding the cities of Mobile, Biloxi and New Orleans as strategic capitals. He and his brother, Pierre Le Moyne d'Iberville, are credited with bringing Mardi Gras to North America.

DEEPWATER HORIZON OIL SPILL

On April 20, 2010, the Deepwater Horizon oil rig exploded, killing 11 workers. The rig leaked nearly five million barrels of crude into the Gulf of Mexico—the largest marine oil spill in history.

Little Maddison Kemp toddled from her mother to her grandmother and back again in the Kemp family room, her polka-dot smock soaked with more juice from the sippy cup than found in her mouth. She was mostly cooing, but occasionally speaking the first words she learned. "Da-da," 14-month-old Maddie said periodically, her arms reaching out to nobody in particular each time she called for her father. But Maddison's calls, as well as those of her 3-year-old sister Kaylee, will never be answered. Roy Wyatt Kemp, the girls' young father, was one of the 11 men killed during the explosion of Transocean's Deepwater Horizon drilling rig. ..."Their daddy and my husband is never coming home," Courtney Kemp said. Soon after the explosion, news accounts were more likely to report on tar balls that might stain the sugar white sand beaches of Alabama and Florida, oiled birds or the impact on Louisiana's delicate marshes than on the 11 men who died on the Deepwater Horizon, which was leased by energy giant BP. A year later that remains true. "These men are all but forgotten except by their families," said Theresa Carpenter, Courtney Kemp's mother who lives less than a mile away from the girls in rural Catahoula Parish where virtually everybody either farms the fertile fields or works in the oil industry. "It seemed like everybody was more worried about the birds than the people," said Courtney's father. Every night when Wyatt was away working on the rig, Courtney and Kaylee would count down the days and then the hours until he was scheduled to arrive home. "He's not coming home," Courtney repeated. "Kaylee cries at night sometimes." ... Steve Newman, Transocean's chief executive, came to the Kemps' home last spring to express condolences. "He said, 'Rest assured, there's nothing to worry about,'" Courtney said. "He'd said we'd be taken care of." Soon after, Courtney said, the company made an offer for compensation. ..."But the offer they made was like spitting in my face." Courtney declined to say what the offer was, although she did say Transocean is continuing to pay Wyatt's salary. BP, she said, has been almost invisible. "The only time I've heard from BP is they sent two representatives to a memorial and two potted plants."
— *Greg Hilburn, USA Today Network, April 11, 2011*

SEASHELLS OF NOTE

Before they wash ashore, seashells serve as the protective exoskeletons of mollusks like clams and snails. Captiva, Sanibel and Marco islands are Florida's most popular beachcombing shores, and the Bailey-Matthews National Shell Museum on Sanibel is the only museum in the U.S. devoted solely to shells. Below, a selection of the most sought-after.

AMERICAN AUGER *Terebridae* Resembles a long thin ice cream cone, with concentric corrugated "whorls," hence its other alias, "many-whorled univalve." Shells come from sea snails shaped like screws with one fearsome, harpoon-like tooth.

....

BROAD-RIBBED CARDITA *Carditamera floridana* Oval clamshell, usually white or gray, has ridges radiating in orange and brown.

....

JUNONIA *Scaphella junonia* Ivory, chignon-shaped shell marked with leopard-like brown dots. Rare as they are beautiful.

....

LION'S PAW *Nodipecten nodosus* Iconic scallop shell known for its fanned shape and knobby, rippled texture. Sunset-colored stripes vary with salmon, pink and purple hues.

....

STIFF PEN SHELL *Atrina rigida* Fish fin silhouette glimmers in iridescent purple or brown. Shells can reach a foot long and sometimes produce black pearls.

....

TRITON'S TRUMPET *Charonia tritonis* Spiraled conch in a pink tortoiseshell motif. Some can grow to 2 feet long.

SHARK TEETH

Beachcombers flock to the Gulf Coast to hunt for fossilized shark teeth that date back 10 million years. Submerged during prehistoric times, present-day Florida was once the floor of an ancient ocean where sharks swam—many in the area of present-day Venice, now known as the "Shark Tooth Capital of the World," where teeth can be found year-round, especially at Manasota Key and Casey Key.

MARDI GRAS

When French colonists settled along the Gulf, they brought with them the Catholic holiday of Mardi Gras, or Fat Tuesday, now observed all along the coast, not just in New Orleans. Below, a sampling of city celebrations.

MOBILE Alabama claims first organized Mardi Gras in the U.S., in 1703. Introduced to Mobile by French-Canadian Le Moyne brothers, who established the city as capital of French Louisiana year prior. The Civil War would stop celebrations, but Joe Cain, a former Confederate soldier and controversial character, credited with reviving them. Even today, Mobile's Mardi Gras events remain mostly racially segregated, subject of the documentary *The Order of Myths*.

BILOXI Mississippi housed the second capital of French Louisiana, in Biloxi, established in 1720. First official celebration occurred 150 years later. On Twelfth Night, Christmas lights on Biloxi lighthouse extinguished and the illumination of Coastal Mississippi Mardi Gras Museum signals the beginning of Carnival season's parades.

NEW ORLEANS Home to most well-known Mardi Gras festivities. New Orleans was named the capital of French Louisiana in 1723, but first organized iterations of Mardi Gras with parades didn't occur until the 1830s. Residents created grand customs, club-like krewes, extravagant floats and society balls. Now city attracts more than 10 million tourists [who can bring the traffic to a standstill for weeks]. State considers Mardi Gras legal holiday.

PENSACOLA While Florida was colonized by the Spanish, Pensacola was captured by the French in 1719 and remained under its control until 1722. First Mardi Gras celebration occurred in 1874 and now considered the third-largest observance in the country. Over 300 pirates march through town during Krewe of Lafitte parade.

Purple, green and gold, the official colors of Mardi Gras, can be seen throughout the region and represent justice, faith and power, respectively.

CITRUS OF NOTE

HONEYBELL TANGELO Heavy-bottomed tangerine-grapefruit cross noted for vibrant, floral sweetness and drip-down-your-arm juiciness.

....

EUREKA LEMON A farmers market find with subtly striped chartreuse and green peel. Tart taste belies its pretty pink interior.

....

CARA CARA ORANGE Coral-colored flesh with low acidity makes for a rosy, easy-sipping glass of OJ.

....

MEYER LEMON Thin-skinned golden globe is mild, honeyed cousin of its conventional counterpart. Namesake founder, botany adventurer Frank Meyer, died shortly after its discovery.

....

CALAMONDIN Small, super sour oranges a favorite in Filipino cooking. Also grown for heady ivory blooms.

....

MEIWA KUMQUAT Sweet rinds and mouth-puckering centers. Mature trees can carry hundreds of these tiny candy-coated orbs.

....

OWARI SATSUMA Ambrosial but tangy. Louisiana's signature citrus is easy to peel, with poppable pieces like a mandarin.

....

MARSH GRAPEFRUIT The first seedless grapefruit is a Florida original known for a pleasant, peachy flavor. Blond precursor to similarly named red and pink offshoots.

....

KEY LIME Not often used in the Gulf Coast's signature pie, as the petite fruit produces only a thimbleful of juice each. Also called bartender's lime.

....

HAMLIN ORANGE Known as a Louisiana Sweet, with sunset-shaded segments. Bountiful branches start to droop in October.

....

DANCY TANGERINE One of the oldest citrus varieties in the country, with Moroccan ancestry. A cross-section reveals a smile of seeds.

....

PONDEROSA LEMON Big and bumpy, their size comes from a pomelo parent mated with a similarly textured citron, the mother fruit of all citrus.

CIGAR FACTORIES

During Tampa's cigar industry boom in the early 1900s, many factory workers couldn't read. Companies hired an orator, "el lector," to read to them, both for entertainment and education, as they rolled cigars. El Lector Honorato Henry Dominguez described the experience in a 1977 Tampa Tribune article.

El lector climbed onto a raised platform, called La Tribuna, usually about halfway along a wall and next to a window, carrying newspapers in Spanish and English. After he got comfortable in his small wooden chair, he began reading the news in Spanish. For about an hour, the reader informed cigarmakers of the world's events. El lector returned to work about one in the afternoon, and read for four half-hour periods, with 15-minute breaks separating each reading "in order to save the voice. After all, we did not have the microphone. In the first period, we read political news from the world over. In the second period, we read news from labor organizations, also the world over. In the third and fourth periods, we read history, novels, culture, entertainment. The great 'Don Quixote' by Cervantes was a favorite. We were more than readers. We were also actors. We read in character. We read to make the characters come alive. We were performers," said Dominguez.

GASPARILLA PIRATES

Every January, Ye Mystic Krewe of Gasparilla stages a flotilla on the Hillsborough River, a tradition dating to 1904. Below, a Morning Tribune article from the same year.

"Ye Mystic Krewe of Gasparilla" will furnish the Carnival feature of the Festival exercises. Gasparilla, a lineal descendant of the famous pirate king who sailed these waters centuries ago, and whose pirate rendezvous is the island of Gasparilla in the Gulf, will come to Tampa, accompanied by his entire retinue. Owing to the necessity of keeping themselves as secure as possible from the prying eyes of government officers, who might take them to task for their repeated depredations upon the raging seas, the Pirate Crew of the Bold Rover of the Southern Main will remain in seclusion until Friday night, when they will appear in full regalia at the Festival Ball at the Tampa Bay Hotel. The costumes of the "Mystic Krewe" bid fair to be the most beautiful ever seen in Tampa and the Pirate-King and his retinue will seem like visitants from another world, suddenly landed in the midst of the bustle and excitement of a modern city.

ZORA NEALE HURSTON

On December 14, 1927, Zora Neale Hurston took a train bound for Plateau, Alabama, to meet Cudjo Lewis. Lewis was believed to be one of the last living passengers of the *Clotilda*, a slave ship that carried an estimated 110 women, men and children from present-day Ghana to Alabama in 1860—53 years after Congress had outlawed the trans-Atlantic slave trade. In 1931, Hurston filed a manuscript that detailed Lewis' story, but Viking Press wouldn't print it without major concessions, which Hurston refused to make. It remained hidden until work by Alice Walker and Valerie Boyd led to its full publication in 2018 as *Barracoon: The Story of the Last "Black Cargo."*

In the introduction, Hurston wrote, "The African slave trade is the most dramatic chapter in the story of human existence. Therefore a great literature has grown up about it. Innumerable books and papers have been written. These are supplemented by the vast lore that has been blown by the breath of inarticulate ones across the seas and lands of the world. Those who justified slaving on various grounds have had their say. Among these are several slave runners who have boasted of their exploits in the contraband flesh. Those who stood aloof in loathing have cried out against it in lengthy volumes."

She continued, "All these words from the seller, but not one word from the sold. The Kings and Captains whose words moved ships. But not one word from the cargo. … Of all the millions transported from Africa to the Americas, only one man is left. He is called Cudjo Lewis and is living at present at Plateau, Alabama, a suburb of Mobile. This is the story of this Cudjo … the only man on earth who has in his heart the memory of his African home; the horrors of a slave raid; the barracoon; the Lenten tones of slavery; and who has sixty-seven years of freedom in a foreign land behind him. How does one sleep with such memories beneath the pillow? How does a pagan live with a Christian God? How has the Nigerian 'heathen' borne up under the process of civilization? I was sent to ask."

> *Mobile-based reporter and documentarian Ben Raines came upon the wreckage of the* Clotilda *during an unusually low tide in 2018. Today, archaeologists and city leaders plan to build a museum to house the schooner's remains in Africatown, a community in Mobile where many of the descendants of the original 110 enslaved people now live.*

JUBILEE

In a phenomenon observed only in two places on earth, Mobile Bay, Alabama, and Tokyo, Japan, fish and crustaceans densely congregate and launch themselves ashore in what is called, on the Gulf, a jubilee. A lack of oxygen in deep waters drives bottom feeders such as blue crab, shrimp, flounder, stingrays and eels into the shallow waters of the bay. Discombobulated by the oxygen deficiency and in a desperate attempt to get it from the air, they either exit the water completely or laze at its edge and gulp. During this natural, yet strange event, massive amounts of sea life gather near the shoreline in a nearly paralyzed state. People run to the beach, pails in hand, to scoop up crabs, fish, shrimp and more. While jubilees cannot be predicted, they usually happen in the summer before sunrise, during a rising tide. And when one occurs, savvy residents nearby rush to the bay with big nets, big buckets and big appetites.

LAFCADIO HEARN

Before finally settling in Japan, Greek-Irish Renaissance man Lafcadio Hearn chronicled New Orleans during the late 1800s. Below, an excerpt from his dispatch "New Orleans in Wet Weather" published in Cincinnati.

Strange it is to observe the approach of one of these eerie fogs, on some fair night. The blue deeps above glow tenderly beyond the sharp crescent of the moon; the heavens seem transformed to an infinite ocean of liquid turquoise, made living with the palpitating life of the throbbing stars. In this limpid clearness, this mellow, tropical moonlight, objects are plainly visible at a distance of miles; far sounds come to the ear with marvelous distinctness—the clarion calls of the boats, the long loud panting of the cotton press, exhaling steamy breath from their tireless lungs of steel. Suddenly sounds become fainter and fainter, as though the atmosphere were made feeble by some unaccountable enchantment; distant objects lose distinctness; the heaven is cloudless, but her lights, low burning and dim, no longer make the night transparent, and a chill falls upon the city, such as augurs the coming of a ghost.

TABASCO

Edmund McIlhenny started selling his Tabasco hot sauce in green wax–sealed
cologne bottles from jungle-like Avery Island, LA, in 1868. A national craze
for the condiment spurred many newspapers across the country to run a
syndicated article about its origin and how to use it. Below, one example.

"TABASCO SAUCE IN ITS OLD LOUISIANA HOME"
The Anaconda Standard
Anaconda, Montana
January 5, 1904

Captain John A. McIlhenny is in the city from Avery island, looking very
much as if he had been on a long military campaign, judging from the rug-
ged, sunburned appearance. ... "There has been a great deal written about
tabasco sauce ever since I can remember. In fact, I think the subject is one
that has been overdone from the newspaper standpoint, and the only new
thing there is about tabasco is the factory. Of course, this was made nec-
essary by the great increase in the business, and it will not be possible for
us to make enough to supply demand." Avery island is perhaps the most
delightful spot in the state, high, dry, and healthful during all seasons of
the year. As Captain McIlhenny states, tabasco has been regarded and
written about as one of the distinct products of Louisiana for more than
half a century. It is almost impossible to get into any first-class hotel or
restaurant anywhere in the United States without finding among the con-
diments tabasco sauce. It is not, however, a sauce that can be used in large
quantities. It is put up in very small bottles and a single drop on an oyster
is all that one can relish. Many funny stories are told of people who enter
New Orleans restaurants and try tabasco on raw oysters for the first time.
They will insist on putting about a teaspoonful on an oyster and gulping
it down, and then the fireworks begin. Such a dose causes the eater to see
all the stars in firmament. A teaspoonful of tabasco would be enough for
a dozen of the largest oysters that ever came out of Bayou creek. Much to
the surprise of those who have so long been familiar with tabasco sauce, all
of the supply of the world's market is raised on about 100 acres of land. But
the manufactured product of this 100 acres is perhaps the most valuable
of any of a like area of land in the United States if not in the world. It has
been said by those who ought to know that the annual net revenues from
tabasco manufacturing were no less than $150,000.

MTV SPRING BREAK

One of the cable channel's spring break pilgrimage sites in the '90s, Panama City Beach once attracted half a million revelers. But one Pensacola News Journal *article describes not-so-good times at the party.*

Comedian Gilbert Gottfried wandered aimlessly around the MTV crew/ press tent, eyeing the seafood salad and asked aloud: "I'm bored, what am I going to do?" It was a sentiment that an estimated 1,500 spring breakers in Panama City Beach had been muttering for hours as they stood sweating underneath a blazing sun. They were waiting to watch an MTV taping of "Get Next To Jenny." "I've been waiting two hours already, and all we've done is listen to some guy telling us when to cheer and how to cheer," said Kevin Stanton, 20, from Florida State University. How were they rewarded? Host Jenny McCarthy interviewed Gottfried and actor Chris Penn for about five minutes each. The two music groups, No Doubt and Cypress Hill, played one song each on a hand-built stage. "I've been to three other MTV spring break specials, and they were much more disgusting. ...This is, well, I don't know. I'm trying to find something to do. It looks like I might have to settle on playing golf with O.J.," said Gottfried.

THE MANGROVE COAST

After retiring to Sarasota, controversial media mogul Karl Bickel commissioned Walker Evans to take photographs for his Gulf history, The Mangrove Coast, *published in 1942. The modern-era images clashed with tales of pirates and conquistadors, yet the book was a hit.*

On the Mangrove Coast, the sun goes down with a calm serenity all its own and special, unstinted pouring out of color on the glistening sand. In the spring it takes but 60 seconds for the great orange ball to slip from sight from the time it first touches the level line of the far horizon until the last tip of its golden circumference disappears. It is a favorite trick of the old-timers, standing on the beach in the evening, to make wagers with the newcomers on the time consumed. It seems much longer. As the sun fades, the evening wears an orchid veil like no other sunset in the world. The coast is calm. But it is a strand littered with great associations. No bastions, no cloistered missions, no monuments to imperial history embellish it. But many great names have passed its way, and though nothing greets the eye, legend is abounding.

VIETNAMESE FISHING COMMUNITIES

When Saigon fell, in 1975, so did the South Vietnamese fishing fleet. Two-thirds of the local fisherfolk abandoned the country, seeking security and refuge elsewhere. Many of the refugees—who numbered nearly 1 million over the next decade—were picked up offshore by American ships and transported to military facilities such as Eglin Air Force Base on the Florida Panhandle. A large amount stayed, establishing themselves along the Gulf Coast, where the climate resembled that of home. While many of these settlers were considered illiterate, they were highly experienced fishers and shrimpers, having spent several generations at sea. With already hard-earned skills, they quickly transitioned into the Gulf's seafood industry. And while natural disasters and seafood imports [often from Vietnam] have hurt the industry in the Gulf of Mexico as of late, the Vietnamese influence is still noticeable in towns like Alabama's Bayou La Batre, where approximately one-third of the population is of Asian descent, and Mobile, where restaurants like Von's Bistro serve bánh mì alongside fried green tomatoes.

LGBTQ+ IN ST. PETERSBURG

Since 2014, St. Petersburg, Florida, has received a perfect score in the Human Rights Campaign's annual Municipal Equality Index, a nationwide assessment of LGBTQ+ support in law, policy and services. The midsize metro's notable longevity on the list of cities supporting equality comes by way of work started much earlier. In 2003, the first St. Pete Pride parade took place a year after the city passed its Human Rights Ordinance to include sexual orientation as a protected status for employment and housing. While then-Mayor Rick Baker did not publicly acknowledge the parade, 10,000 people flooded the streets to celebrate unity. The parade has since grown into Florida's largest Pride celebration, and in the intervening years, St. Petersburg's current mayor Rick Kriseman [the only city council member in 2003 who supported the Pride parade], has created an LGBTQ+ liaison in the police force; a dedicated mental health facility, the Sunshine Center; and a welcome center for LGBTQ+ visitors. The most visible symbol of St. Petersburg's mission of inclusion can be found at 25th Street and Central Avenue, where a multicolored mural honoring the Pride flag, the trans flag and people of color stretches across the intersection.

ROSEWOOD MASSACRE

One of the more horrific race-related killings in U.S. history is also one of the least known. Renewed interest in the 1923 attack has brought a tiny Florida town and its community back into view.

On January 1, 1923, before the first arcs of light poured in through the cypress stands surrounding Rosewood, Florida [a then-affluent Black community of roughly 350 residents], there was little sense that the promise of a new year was about to turn. When a white woman in the neighboring town of Sumner claimed she'd been assaulted by Rosewood resident Jesse Hunter, a mob followed the railroad to fellow resident Aaron Carrier's home, where Hunter was believed to be. They murdered Hunter and tied Carrier to a car, dragging him back to Sumner. Over the following days, the gang proceeded to hang Sam Carter from an oak, riddling his body with bullets. They also executed James Carrier, after first forcing him to dig his own gravestone. As the state remained silent, newspaper coverage emboldened the mob, and soon men from all over the state arrived in Rosewood and killed any Black person they saw. By January 6, not a single structure in the town stood, save the home of a white man who hid his Black neighbors from the mob. The town was gone, set on fire and left a pile of ash. Those residents who survived hid in the swamps for days until they were rescued by a passing train. The bodies of those slain by the mob remained in the woods of Levy County. The death toll is still unknown. Law enforcement made no arrests, and the media took little interest in recounting the story of Rosewood until decades later, when Gary Moore, a reporter for the *St. Petersburg Times,* shed light on the history in a 1982 story. A decade later, the state completed its own investigation and began the process of paying reparations to descendants. As Moore wrote, "Rosewood stands as a symbol of the countless secret deaths and tortures that took place in an era that has slipped from view."

Florida legislators passed reparations legislation to benefit the descendants of Rosewood victims in 1994. According to a 2020 Tampa Bay Times *article, the state gave $150,000 payments to nine individuals and created the Rosewood Family Scholarship for academic tuition. "In America, as an African American, I do feel that reparations are definitely warranted," said Ebony Pickett, one of the recipients quoted in the story. "Rosewood is a great example that it can definitely be done."*

HURRICANES OF NOTE

Some of the most memorable storms to hit the Gulf on recent record.

Camille *August 1969*	The Category 5 is the second-strongest hurricane to ever hit the U.S. It brought a 24-foot storm surge to southern Mississippi and caused fatal flooding in Appalachia, where it crossed over as a tropical storm.
Elena *August 1985*	The quickly formed storm drew a volatile line through the Gulf, stalling off Cedar Key, before making landfall near Biloxi as a Category 3. Elena led to the evacuation of more than 1 million.
Charley *August 2004*	After making landfall as a Category 4 west of Fort Myers, Charley marched up the coast into Florida's citrus belt, decimating the groves and isolating some rural towns from emergency services.
Ivan *September 2004*	For three weeks, Ivan haunted the Caribbean, the Gulf and even America's Eastern Seaboard as a Category 5 before making landfall as a 3 along the Florida–Alabama border. Inside Ivan's eyewall, the wave height reached 131 feet.
Katrina *August 2005*	The infamous storm left an indelible mark on the entire coast, from Louisiana to Florida, as a Cat 5, but its legacy is bound up in the bones of New Orleans, where the levees failed and the city flooded. In the end, 1,800 people across the Gulf died.
Michael *October 2018*	Michael leveled Mexico Beach, Florida, as a Category 5 storm. In its wake, stands of trees were splintered as if an eraser had been dragged up from the coast.
Laura *August 2020*	Preceded Marco by nine days, Laura hit southwest Louisiana as a Category 4 and killed 42 people despite warnings of "unsurvivable" storm surge.

Hurricanes weren't named until the late 1940s. Today, the World Meteorological Organization recycles names from a set list and retires ones associated with massively damaging or deadly storms.

EUGENE WALTER

Commonly referred to as "Mobile's Renaissance Man," Eugene Walter spent the 20th century crisscrossing the globe and spinning tall tales fashioned from his Alabama upbringing. The bohemian grew up in the Azalea City, where he befriended a young Truman Capote, then spent his adult life in Greenwich Village, New York, and abroad, always carrying with him a shoebox full of Alabama red clay to remind him of home. Fluent in French, Spanish and Italian, Walter relocated to France in the 1950s and, alongside George Plimpton, helped launch *The Paris Review*. In the 1960s, he settled in Rome, where he acted in classic films such as $8\frac{1}{2}$, composed musical scores and translated for directors, including Federico Fellini. He was also known to gather luminaries like William Faulkner and Judy Garland around his dinner table. He returned to Mobile in 1979 and spent the rest of his days cooking, drawing and regularly performing readings. In one memorable speech, he lamented the end of "porch life," which he blamed on the invention of air conditioning. The city granted Walter special permission to be buried in Church Street Graveyard.

> "*Down in Mobile, they're all crazy, because the Gulf Coast is the kingdom of monkeys, the land of clowns, ghosts and musicians, and Mobile is sweet lunacy's county seat.*" —*Eugene Walter,* The Untidy Pilgrim [1954]

STETSON KENNEDY

Folklorist and activist Stetson Kennedy wrote about the Gulf Coast while employed with the Florida Writers' Project, an offshoot program of the Works Progress Administration. Below, a passage from his 1942 book, Palmetto Country, *what Stetson called a "barefoot social history" of the state.*

The Palmetto Country is literally overrun with practitioners of the occult. Florida, in particular, is plagued with almost as many as that other haven for all things other-worldly, California. Leaving aside the more respectable and accepted sects like the Christian Scientists, Seventh Day Adventists, Jehovah's Witnesses, Holy Rollers, and so on, the region is a seventh heaven for everything from fortune-tellers with a deck of cards to palmists, astrologers, crystal-gazers, soothsayers, spiritualists, root doctors, and other voodoo groups.

SMUGGLERS

JEAN AND PIERRE LAFITTE French pirate brothers, the Lafittes ran the pirate stronghold of Barataria Bay, where stolen goods were sold before they were smuggled into New Orleans. Lafitte-linked privateers plotted a failed scheme to steal Pensacola from the Spanish and turn it into a pirate haven.

....

AL CAPONE The Chicago gangster was said to have purchased properties around St. Petersburg, during the land boom of the 1920s. Newspaper accounts from the time noted Scarface visiting Tarpon Springs and other parts of Pinellas County to expand his rum-running operations.

....

WALTER P. FULLER The Florida author, historian and legislator was a noted bootlegger, using his swanky Jungle Country Club Hotel in St. Petersburg as a cover. He wrote a letter to a local newspaper admitting 20 members of Al Capone's gang had stayed at his hotel.

PINECRAFT

The Amish and Mennonite snowbird community in Florida has been active since the 1920s, when many followers were encouraged to farm celery around Sarasota to avoid harsh New England winters. Below, an article detailing Pinecraft's warm allure.

Ah, you say, but wintering in Florida? Isn't that a vanity? Sitting on his screened-in porch in late afternoon, Henry Miller ponders the question, then smiles through his Amish beard and tells you: "God created the whole earth. This is just a place to go where the climate is more comfortable." Getting to Florida can be a tough proposition if you own only a horse and buggy. But strict Amish like the Millers manage. They help pay expenses down with a Mennonite neighbor who owns a car or they take a train or bus. Their entertainment is limited by their conservative beliefs, but they enjoy their Florida winters. There are four Mennonite churches in Sarasota now. And the Amish hold their services in the home of one of the members. "As we look back over these years," wrote Walter Ebersole, a trustee of one of the churches, in a church magazine, "we can say with the poet, 'God moves in a mysterious way. His wonders to perform.' He has always opened the way when we hardly knew what would happen next."

—Asbury Park Evening Press, *Asbury, New Jersey, April 25, 1961*

SEMINOLES

For more than 14,000 years the Native peoples of Florida's Gulf Coast—the Uzita on the Little Manatee River and the Calusa and Creek—thrived in stable, undisturbed societies. But in May 1513, Juan Ponce de León entered Charlotte Harbor at the mouth of the Myakka River. There, Spanish colonists made contact with the Calusa in a grim exchange of fire. They returned in 1521, but their two ships were driven away in bloodshed. An arrowhead pierced Ponce de León's thigh, though he made it to Havana before he died from the injury. [As the poet William Carlos Williams put it, the Calusa had "let his fountain out."] In 1821, the Seminole Wars bookended Spain's cession of Florida to the United States, and in 1823, the Treaty of Moultrie Creek robbed the tribes of their land and confined them to a U.S.-controlled reservation. It was in this same period, the individual tribes lost their names and, over time, became collectively known as Seminoles. Under the umbrella of that name, the tribes migrated into an impenetrable fortress of grass fom Lake Okeechobee to Florida Bay, later named the Everglades, and the Seminoles lived there peacefully until developers bisected their haven with the Tamiami Trail, now a highway that connects Tampa to Miami.

SPONGE DIVING

Tarpon Springs, Florida, has the highest Greek American population of any U.S. city. Immigrants arriving in the 1880s built a robust industry harvesting and exporting sponges from the Gulf. A 1904 *Miami News* article explains the sponge-diving process like this: "The actual sponging is done from rowboats or very small vessels, the hooker using a three pronged rake 30 or 40 feet long and with the aid of a water pail—an ordinary water bucket with a glass bottom—readily detects and detaches sponges from the bottom. ... The sponges when first obtained are far from what we are accustomed to see at stores. They are full of animal matter, and this must be allowed to die and then dried and hammered out and finally detached. Sponges are auctioned off to the dealers [and] distributed all over the country and even in Great Britain, the Netherlands, Belgium and France." Not as many people know the role Black spongers played in Tarpon Springs' development. According to a 1990 *Tampa Tribune-Times* story, "A portion of St. Nicholas Greek Orthodox Cathedral was paid for by Black spongers. When the Greek sponge fishermen donated the first four or five sponges from their catch to pay for the cathedral, Black spongers pitched in too."

LENA RICHARD

*While Cajun chef Paul Prudhomme might be more known for using
television to popularize Louisiana cooking, New Orleans chef and caterer
Lena Richard's network program debuted in 1949, nearly 50 years before
Prudhomme's PBS series. The first Black woman to host her own TV show,
she was also the first Black author of a Creole cookbook, the recipes of which
were the focus of her on-air tutorials. Below, the gumbo filé from her* New
Orleans Cook Book, *which she served at her restaurant Gumbo House, one
of few Black-owned fine-dining restaurants in the city during segregation.*

GUMBO FILÉ

1 cup chopped chicken meat	3 teaspoons filé
2 ¹/₂ quarts chicken stock	1 medium sized onion
¹/₂ dozen crabs	1 clove of garlic
1 pound lake shrimp	3 tablespoons flour
¹/₂ pound or 1 slice raw ham	4 tablespoons cooking oil
1 bay leaf	Salt and pepper to taste

Fry ham and shrimp in cooking oil until ham is a golden brown. Remove
ham and shrimp from fat. Make a roux with flour and fat, add onions and
cook until a golden brown. Add crabs, chicken, ham and shrimp, stock and
all seasonings except salt and pepper. Cook over a slow fire until liquid has
reduced to about 1 ¹/₂ quarts. Season with salt and pepper and, just before
serving, stir in filé. It is customary to serve Gumbo Filé with rice.

---

*One of the chefs most associated with Gulf Coast cooking hails from
an entirely different seaboard. Emeril Lagasse was born in Fall
River, Massachusetts, and came to New Orleans at just 23 years old
to succeed Prudhomme as executive chef at the famed Commander's
Palace. After opening his own restaurant, he brought Creole and
Cajun cooking to the masses by way of his Food Network shows,*
The Essence of Emeril *and* Emeril Live. *His gravelly baritone
exclamation, "Bam!" endeared him to a national audience and
launched him as one of the first mega-celebrity chefs.*

RINGLING BROS.

When the Florida land boom collapsed in 1927, John Ringling brought the
winter headquarters of his Ringling Bros. and Barnum & Bailey Circus
to Sarasota to save the city's economy. Below, a 1927 Tampa Daily Times
article, the day before the winter headquarters opened on Christmas.

Completed, the headquarters have become a regular little city, with virtually a small town population. The buildings include a dining hall, wagon works, mill, car shops, elephant house, horse corral, bareback riders training quarters, electricians shops, wardrobe department, harness making shops, camel and zebra sheds, sleeping quarters, and hospital, at the head of which is Dr. William G. Shields, circus physician. It means that the entire winter headquarters have been transplanted from Bridgeport, Conn., to Sarasota. It is unnecessary to give the long list of jungle animals housed in the menagerie. The principal interest is in seeing the manner in which they spend their winters. Besides the wide variety of members of the cat family, among which is "Whitey," the largest tiger in captivity, there are several members of the oryx species, the hippos, kangaroos, tapirs, and many others. Forty elephants are housed in the barns built for them. The circus also possesses 750 horses which are now in the corrals.

TARPON

"Catching a Huge Fish"
The New York Times, May 2, 1886

An immense tarpon, the largest game fish ever captured, was exhibited yesterday in the window of Thomas J. Conroy's fishing tackle store. It was caught at Punta Rassa. Fla., by William H. Wood, a civil engineer of this city and an expert angler. The fish is 6 feet 5 inches in length, 16 ¹/₂ inches in width, and weighs 140 pounds. A 15-thread reel line, a hook with the O'Shaughnessy knob and 3-foot link chain, and a short stiff bamboo rod in one piece, with 900 feet of line, were used. The fish showed such tremendous strength that there was great difficulty in beaching it, and this was only accomplished finally by lifting anchor and allowing it to tow the boat ashore. Mr. Wood enjoys the additional distinction of being the first person who ever captured a fish of this kind with rod and reel.

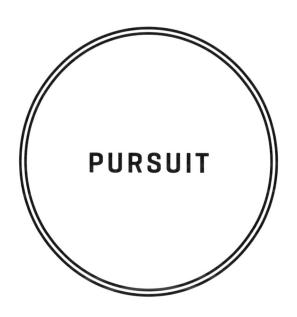

PURSUIT

———

A field guide to Gulf Coast seafood from catch to plate with historical background, cultural insight, fishing advice and a curated selection of the best seafood spots in the region

SEAFOOD HISTORY

The formation of America's ancient sea provided the ingredients for abundant waters and massive industry. A mélange of cultures and traditions merging over centuries—in addition to generations of fishers, shrimpers and oyster farmers— created one of the country's most unique and admired culinary canons.

FOUNDATIONS

CULTURE

Indigenous tribes called the coast home for thousands of years prior to European colonizers. Groups like the Calusa were notably not nomadic, as the Gulf provided an endless bounty year-round. The Spanish arrived in the early 1500s, quickly followed by the French and British and, then, the ensuing trans-Atlantic slave trade, which brought thousands of West African people to the coast. Out of these diverse groups, among others, emerged Creole people and cultural customs within music, religion and especially food—embodied in seafood dishes from gumbo to paella.

CLIMATE

Climatologists classify most of the shoreline as a humid subtropical region, comparable to areas like southern Brazil. The Gulf's bathtub-warm waters are a haven for shrimp and migrating fish. Hurricanes, floods and oppressive humidity plague every inch of the coast, creating a trying and often dangerous environment for seafood workers. Rising sea levels and unpredictable temperatures contribute to species and landscape loss.

GEOLOGY

The Gulf's formation began 200 million years ago when the Yucatán Peninsula split from what is now Florida during the breakup of Pangea. As dinosaurs roamed and water levels rose and fell, the Gulf shrank into its current 600,000-square-mile footprint fringed by bays, estuaries, rivers and streams. Jurassic-age mineral deposits provide the roux for the Gulf's merroir—much like terroir, but expressed in seafood. It's most specifically understood in oysters that possess tasting notes as varied as cucumber, fresh buttermilk, citrus and shiitake mushroom.

TIMELINE

1513 ...... Spaniard Juan Ponce de León leads expedition to the coast of what is now Florida

1682 ..... Frenchman Henri de Tonti reaches mouth of Mississippi River, claims surrounding territory for Louis the Great

1718 ..... Jean-Baptiste Le Moyne founds New Orleans

1735 ...... France exports seines [large nets] to Louisiana Cajuns for catching white shrimp

1860 .... Steam-powered Florida Railroad completed, connects Atlantic Ocean to Gulf of Mexico

1861 ..... Civil War debilitates transportation infrastructure, economy

1868 .... World's first commercial ice plant opens in New Orleans, transforms storage

1881 ..... Louisville & Nashville Railroad purchase connects port cities of Mobile and New Orleans. First oyster and shrimp cannery opens in Biloxi, processing and packing, becomes largest in world

1903 ..... Biloxi gains reputation as the Seafood Capital of the World

1913 ...... Boats now equipped with power-operated dredges, maximizing oyster harvests

1917 ..... Modern gas or diesel engines replace sails on fishing boats

...... Introduction of otter trawls expands fishing range, cuts manpower

1975 ..... Fleeing war, Vietnamese refugees resettle on Gulf Coast and enter seafood business

1986 ..... Winston Groom's fictional Forrest Gump becomes shrimp boat captain in Bayou La Batre

2005 .... Hurricane Katrina makes landfall; production losses cost seafood industry $1.5 billion

2010 .... Deepwater Horizon drilling rig explodes, spilling 4.9 million barrels of oil. NOAA bans commercial and recreational fishing in affected waters for months

.... First Gulf commercial oyster farms start up in Alabama and Louisiana

2014 .... Louisiana shrimpers go on strike, citing cheap imports

2020 .... Apalachicola Bay temporarily closes oyster bed appellations to restore estuary

GULF COAST FISH

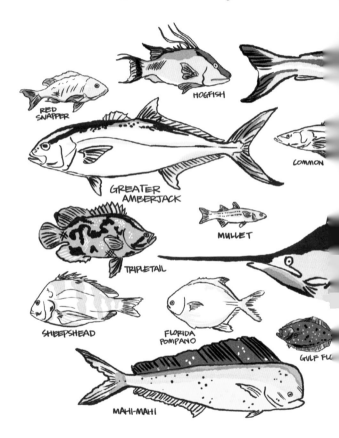

RED
SNAPPER

HOGFISH

GREATER
AMBERJACK

COMMON

MULLET

TRIPLETAIL

SHEEPSHEAD

FLORIDA
POMPANO

GULF FLO

MAHI-MAHI

PECIES OF NOTE

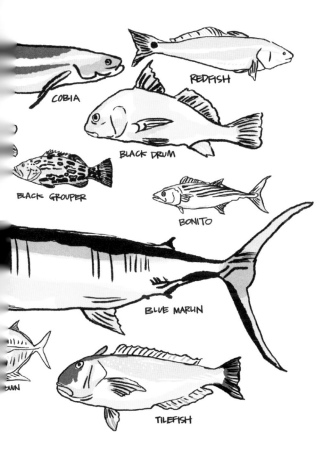

COBIA

REDFISH

BLACK DRUM

BLACK GROUPER

BONITO

BLUE MARLIN

OWN

TILEFISH

FISH SPECIES

A survey of the best catches for the table.

Black Drum	Ash-colored fish named for the noise it creates when it contracts air bladder. Can reach 90 pounds.
Black Grouper	Prized for firm, subtly sweet fillets without pin bones. Grouper fingers are a Gulf delicacy.
Blue Marlin	Pointy-nosed icon of mantelpiece and literature [*The Old Man and the Sea*]. Tastes similar to swordfish.
Cobia	Wild specimens can weigh up to 150 pounds. A newcomer to seafood menus, especially cobia collars.
Common Snook	Popular game fish hides in mangrove estuaries. Carnivorous, it feasts on shrimp and crustaceans.
Florida Pompano	The Goldilocks of fish with a buttery, crowd-pleasing taste and edible skin.
Greater Amberjack	Can reach 6 feet in length. Like a mood ring, fish's side stripe gets darker when it's excited or eating.
Hogfish	Tangerine-hued. Can grow to match size of state fair–winning pig. Uses snout to root in the sand for food.
Lookdown	Long-faced sliver of silver. Congregates in small schools by bridges and sandy areas.
Mullet	Called "Biloxi bacon" but more so the pride of Florida. Rich and oily, stays moist and firm even when smoked.
Redfish	Found in shallow flats and lagoons. Populations being rebuilt due to overfishing.
Red Snapper	Ask for this coral-colored, longline-caught fish by name [impostors abound].
Tripletail	Three rounded fins point backward. Floats on one side near surface to mimic leaves or debris.

FISHING GUIDES

*Experienced experts on the best catches from their
respective corners of the coast.*

THE GUIDE: TY HIBBS   **THE CATCH:** REDFISH

"People who aren't from here think, 'Holy crap, everything looks the same.' But I've passed every blade of grass in this state and I've never seen anyplace where you can drive 10 miles and be in such different terrain. On the water, you can go from a sandy beach to oyster flats to muddy marsh and then solid river water and 10-foot-tall roseau cane. If you head out one of the passes around Venice, you can be in blue water in a matter of a few minutes." *Venice, LA* [504] 343-9017

....

THE GUIDE: MELANIE GANNON   **THE CATCH:** SNOOK

"Spring through summer is my favorite time of year because the snook start pushing out onto the beaches, and there are just so many opportunities for sight fishing, especially for beginners. The water is just crystal clear, and you can find yourself walking miles of empty beaches with big groups of fish sliding along the shore. There are no mangrove roots or structure, so it makes for a perfect way to target snook." *Sarasota, FL* [941] 256-6859

....

THE GUIDE: RICHARD SCHMIDT   **THE CATCH:** BLACK DRUM

"There aren't many people doing what I do, sight fishing for reds and black drum, so I have a lot of spots to myself. In spring, we can find 50 or 60 fish in a pod, which is great for the novice angler. It's a target-rich environment. In summer, there's such a variety around the barrier islands—big sea trout, huge jacks and tripletail. In the fall, it's good everywhere—the Biloxi Marsh, Pass Christian and the Chandeleur Islands." *Gulfport, MS richardschmidtflyfishing.com*

....

THE GUIDE: LACEY KELLY   **THE CATCH:** TARPON [CENTRAL COAST]

"Up in the swamp, a lot of people step up on the bow and say, 'I've just never seen so many tarpon in such a small area.' It's almost like you can walk across their backs in every direction. We have migratory fish that when they get into Homosassa, up into the Nature Coast, they have some different behavior. When they get to the swamp, they just want to take a breather and rest." *Homosassa, FL floridaoutdoorexperience.com*

GEAR

SPIN ROD & REEL

St. Croix Triumph 7'6" Medium
Fin-Nor Lethal LT430
Ready-for-anything kit for any skill level

FLY ROD & REEL

Temple Fork Outfitters BVK Nine
Waterworks-Lamson Liquid Reel
Stretch line without stretching your budget

PLIERS

Cheeky Fishing 750
*Lightweight snippers. Slice saltwater
line quickly*

FIELD KNIFE

Coutelier NOLA
New Orleans shop carries best makers

FISHING NET

Heart Wood Trade
Handcarved wooden handles

OUTERWEAR

Tom Beckbe Tensaw Jacket
Sleeves designed for full range of motion

HIP PACK

Topo Designs Quick Pack
Keeps flies, phone, tools handy and secure

COOLER

YETI Hopper Flip 12
Works as dry bag too

SUNGLASSES

Costa Del Mar Sport Performance Frames
Polarized lenses protect eyes from water's glare

SUN PROTECTION

Buff CoolNet UV+
*Prevents burn without sunscreen chemicals
that damage marine life*

OUTFITTERS

239 FLIES
Bonita Springs, FL

AMI OUTFITTERS
Anna Maria Island, FL

APALACH OUTFITTERS
Apalachicola, FL

BILL JACKSON'S
SHOP FOR ADVENTURE
Pinellas Park, FL

BOCA GRANDE OUTFITTERS
Boca Grande, FL

ECONOMY TACKLE
Sarasota, FL

MASSEY'S PROFESSIONAL
OUTFITTERS
New Orleans, LA

NELSON OUTDOORS
Pascagoula, MS

OLD FLORIDA OUTFITTERS
Santa Rosa Beach, FL

RED BEARD'S OUTFITTER
Mobile, AL

TAILWATER OUTFITTERS
Palm Harbor, FL

TAMPA FISHING OUTFITTERS
Tampa, FL

WHITNEY'S BAIT & TACKLE
Sanibel Island, FL

CULTURES OF NOTE

The myriad groups that created the Gulf Coast's foodways.

French	Those direct-from-France and Acadians of Canada [Cajuns] lent both cosmopolitan and country cooking techniques, bisque to boucherie.
Spanish	Spaniards brought peaches and citrus over to the new-to-them world, as well as rice dishes like paella, which also led to jambalaya.
West African	Labor and ingenuity of enslaved people, free people and their descendants, including creoles of color, form foundation of Gulf food traditions. Some in seafood: gumbo, court bouillon, barbecue shrimp.
Greek	One of the largest Greek-American communities grew up around the sponge-diving industry in Central Florida. Already accustomed to a Mediterranean diet, they took quickly to Gulf seafood.
Caribbean	Cubans and Haitians, already influenced by French and Spanish colonization, came to Gulf with previous generation of Creole recipes and ingredients from crab to coffee, flan to field peas.
Italian	Most Italian immigrants, specifically Sicilians, arrived in late 1800s, many working in seafood canning and levee building. New Orleans oyster bars, Felix's and Acme, founded by Italians.
Vietnamese	During the United States conflict in Vietnam, refugees, already skilled as fishers, settled along the Gulf and became integral part of seafood industry. Cơm gà, bánh mì and pho pervasive on the coast.
Latin American	Workers from Latin America rebuilt Gulf cities after Hurricane Katrina. Southeast Louisiana is home to largest population of Hondurans outside the Central American country. Seafood dishes to note: coctel de camarones, ceviche, escabeche.

ESSENTIAL SEAFOOD DISHES

Beyond the fried basket. Key recipes and cookbooks to study.

SEAFOOD GUMBO

Creole cornerstone. Typically made with chocolate-colored roux, okra or filé powder for thickener, and plenty of oysters, crab and shrimp. *The Dooky Chase Cookbook*

CRAWFISH BOIL

Come spring, pots spill spicy combo of crawfish, potatoes, corn and sausage onto tables. Vietnamese revolutionized Cajun formula. *Real Cajun: Rustic Home Cooking From Donald Link's Louisiana*

WEST INDIES SALAD

Credited to Mobile Bay restaurant owner Bill Bayley, who as merchant mariner in the Caribbean picked up idea for chilled crabmeat with oil, vinegar and sliced onion. *Recipe Jubilee!: Junior League of Mobile*

CHARGRILLED OYSTERS

Oysters cooked over a fire in shell with butter, cheese, breadcrumbs and herbs. Go by the names of Bienville, Rockefeller, etc. *Good Catch: Recipes & Stories Celebrating the Best of Florida's Waters*

DEVIL CRAB

Cuban croquettes. Blue crab meat simmered in spicy sofrito sauce, shaped into footballs and deep-fried. *Clarita's Cocina*

SHRIMP PASTA

Italian-American innovation easily adapted to wherever immigrants settled. On the Gulf, shrimp are often swaddled in lemon-garlic or tomato sauce over nest of spaghetti. *Shrimp: A Savor the South Cookbook*

MULLET DIP

Smoked fillets whipped up with mayo, cream cheese, pickle relish, celery, green onions, lemon and hot sauce. *The Florida Cookbook: From Gulf Coast Gumbo to Key Lime Pie*

BLACKENED REDFISH

Cajun chef Paul Prudhomme's creation so popular in '70s it caused Gulf fishery closing. Butter-dipped fillets coated in spices form thick crust in hot skillet. *Chef Paul Prudhomme's Louisiana Kitchen*

GRILLED OCTOPUS

Oft-seen in Florida's Greek restaurants. Tentacles grilled till tender. Served with olive oil and lemon. *Louis Pappas' Famous Greek Recipes*

SEAFOOD PAELLA

A Spanish classic. Bomba rice simmers in a wide, shallow pan with peppers, onions, tomatoes, garlic, spices and white wine. Dotted with clams, shrimp, scallops. *The Columbia Restaurant Spanish Cookbook*

FISH

TED PETERS FAMOUS SMOKED FISH
St. Petersburg, FL
Smoking mullet, mahi-mahi, salmon and mackerel over red oak since 1951.

WALT'Z FISH SHAK
Madeira Beach, FL
Funky fish camp perched over John's Pass and turquoise water. The move: yellowedge grouper.

BILLY'S SEAFOOD
Bon Secour, AL
Open-air market right on the docks of fishing village Bon Secour. Whole snapper on ice.

STAR FISH COMPANY MARKET
Cortez, FL
Old Florida gem looking out on Anna Maria Island. Order the Florida pompano alongside hush puppies and slaw.

BOZO'S SEAFOOD MARKET
Pascagoula, MS
Longtime lunch counter has primo fish dinners too. The Wahozo has two thick, blackened wahoo fillets.

MINERAL SPRINGS SEAFOOD
Panacea, FL
The myth, the legend: the Hot Mess. A dip made from smoked tuna, cobia and salmon.

SHRIMP

MANCI'S ANTIQUE CLUB
Daphne, AL
Tchotchke-strewn Beatnik dive often has live music. Shrimp po'boy, dressed, with sidewinder fries.

THORNY OYSTER
Bay Saint Louis, MS
Hip hotel raw bar pairs Royal Reds, white shrimp's coral-colored cousin, with chile-ginger butter.

SANDBAR RESTAURANT
Anna Maria Island, FL
Shrimp and gnocchi or peel-and-eats dunked in cocktail sauce. Can't go wrong.

ST. JOE SHRIMP COMPANY
Cape San Blas, FL
Pick up a Styrofoam clamshell filled with spicy shrimp boil. Eat it on the tailgate at the beach.

DELCAMBRE SEAFOOD
Delcambre, LA
Dockside gathering where parishioners from Vietnamese church St. Andrew Dung-Lac serve fried shrimp and spring rolls.

MR. SHRIMP
New Orleans, LA
On speed dial for many Crescent City residents. Doorstep-delivers pounds of crazy fresh, colossal U10s.

OYSTER

HOLE IN THE WALL
Apalachicola, FL

Make friends with Barbara. She'll cut you a good piece of her Key lime pie after a dozen on the half shell.

....

WINTZELL'S OYSTER HOUSE
Mobile, AL

Rockefeller, Bienville, Monterey and chargrilled all present on the sampler platter at Mobile's original 1938 outpost.

....

FRENCH HERMIT OYSTER CO.
Deer Island, MS

Mike Arguelles operates stronger-together co-op with other farmers like Tommy Nguyen of Saint Ella Oyster Co.

....

LYNN'S QUALITY OYSTERS
Eastpoint, FL

Sits on a bucolic edge of the Forgotten Coast. Lynn Martina has been shucking since she was 9.

....

PASCAL'S MANALE
New Orleans, LA

A 1913 relic. Happy hour here sees all kinds of characters.

....

BLUEGILL RESTAURANT
Spanish Fort, AL

An old Mobile Bay haunt on a pier. Oysters roasted over a bed of flames.

CRAB

THE PINK ELEPHANT
Boca Grande, FL

Midcentury glam with flamingo umbrellas over philodendron fronds. Dip stone crab claws in smoky Louis sauce.

....

WESTWEGO SHRIMP LOT
Westwego, LA

Gravel patch where Louisiana seafood vendors hawk the best.

....

COLUMBIA RESTAURANT
Ybor City, FL

Oldest restaurant in Florida [116 years running] continues to cook up Spanish-Cuban staples like devil crab croquettes.

....

TASTY TAILS SEAFOOD
Biloxi, MS

Whole blue crabs sautéed in Thai-basil-garlic-butter sauce.

....

MOSQUITO SUPPER CLUB
New Orleans, LA

Coastal Cajun cooking in the city. She-crab bisque, marinated crab claws, fried soft-shells, the list goes on.

....

SHELLY'S SEAFOOD MARKET
Homosassa, FL

Smith family sells blue and stone crabs direct from their boat in a gray barn under Spanish moss–cloaked oaks.

PERSPECTIVES

"One of the best things that can happen when I'm traveling is someone inviting me into their home and cooking for me. In the beginning, I was trying to chase the flavor of the food I ate growing up in the fishing village of Chauvin and cook it exactly how my mom did. I was inviting people into her kitchen through me in New Orleans. We still serve this traditional Cajun food but we evolve it. We can also show people where all this seafood comes from and the community they're supporting all at one meal."

—MELISSA MARTIN, owner and chef of Mosquito Supper Club [*New Orleans, LA*]

"Our goal at Fisher's is to keep Alabama seafood in Alabama. Red snapper is one of the most delicate, beautiful fish we have, and the state does a great job of protecting it. Next door, Bayou La Batre is heaven when it comes to crabmeat. And Alabama shrimp, they're just the best."

—BILL BRIAND, executive chef of Fisher's at Orange Beach Marina [*Orange Beach, AL*]

"My farm is based in Wakulla County. Wakulla means 'mysterious waters.' Our bay, Oyster Bay, is really unique because it's fed by a bunch of springs straight from Florida's aquifer. I only take out of the water what I can put back in. Over time, these oysters eat up all the algae and nitrogen to grow their shells so they're purifying this water at the same time. Because of that, a lot of keystone species like sheepshead, mullet and stone crabs are coming back."

—CAINNON GREGG, owner of Pelican Oyster Company [*Wakulla County, FL*]

"If you look around, there aren't many folks that own their own fishing excursion business that look like me. Growing up, I watched fishing shows all the time, but I never saw anybody I could relate to doing this. I want to create a more diverse fishing industry, and the team we've assembled is definitely intentional in that. But we're also all friends who just love to fish."

—LIONEL JAMES, fishing captain and owner of Lion's Tale Adventures [*Destin, FL*]

INTERVIEWS

Ten conversations with locals of note about gumbo, mermaids, photography, farmworkers, climate change, Mardi Gras, bayous, bobcats and more

JACK E. DAVIS

HISTORIAN

GROWING UP, the Gulf was central to my sense of place. It shaped my understanding of the world.

MY LIFE REVOLVED around water—being on it, being in it, being under it.

I SPENT FIVE years in the Navy. Even though I was on the Atlantic, I missed the Gulf. There was something absent from my life. Something that I wanted to get back to.

WHEN I STARTED writing *The Gulf* in 2010, my mind cast back to my childhood on Santa Rosa Sound and the beaches in the Tampa Bay area.

WHEN I WROTE about the coast, I was getting to know its biography and thinking about it as a living place, almost like a person. Once the book came out, my relationship with the Gulf moved to a whole other level.

IT'S REALLY HARD to describe, this profound feeling of something like a rebirth.

I WITNESSED WHAT happened throughout the '80s and '90s in bringing these estuarine environments back to life. I watched the fish come back, the birds. It gives me hope because we've done it once.

WE CAN DO it again.

I THINK WE'RE doing it again now—restoring the living shorelines around the Gulf. They're our best defense against sea-level rise.

AS WALTER ANDERSON used to say, he felt like a privileged spectator being in the presence of all this life during his trips to the barrier islands off Mississippi and Louisiana.

THAT'S HOW I feel when I'm alone anywhere on the Gulf Coast, whether it's just floating around the Cedar Keys at a time of day where you don't see or hear anybody. Or standing on the Louisiana Marsh.

I JUST FEEL really privileged to be there.

VIRGINIA HANUSIK

PHOTOGRAPHER

I GREW UP in the Hudson River Valley, a very iconic landscape in the American art canon.

THERE'S A SIGNIFICANT lack of artwork or visuals from the Gulf taught in American art courses or appreciated on the same level.

MY ACADEMIC BACKGROUND is in architecture. I took a photography class to fulfill an art requirement.

I FOUND OUT I could express myself and think about the built environment in this different context.

I MOVED TO New Orleans for an organization working on coastal restoration in South Louisiana. I used photography to orient myself in this landscape and understand these complex issues around climate change happening here.

THE DOMINANT IMAGES of climate change are around disasters. Those photos build a violent, severe narrative around climate change.

THAT'S NOT what people are experiencing on a day-to-day basis here.

WE HAVE A unique connection with water here. It's embedded in every aspect of our lives and culture.

WITH MY infrastructure photos, sometimes you're looking at a frickin' levee wall. It's cement or grass.

HOW DO YOU make that interesting? I rely on natural light a lot.

I'M TRYING TO show the systems that make life possible here. It's a very human-engineered landscape. These structures are also symbols that represent choosing to protect certain communities over others.

IT SOUNDS so cheesy, but I had a genuinely grounding, spiritual experience at the very end of the Mississippi River in Port Eads, Louisiana, which is only accessible by boat.

AT SUNSET, it's completely breathtaking. There are no words to describe it.

CRAIG PITTMAN

JOURNALIST

I'M FROM PENSACOLA and came to St. Pete in 1989 for a job at the *St. Petersburg Times,* now the *Tampa Bay Times.*

THE PANHANDLE IS so interesting because it's the Bible Belt, but it's also a port. So you've got this weird mix of conservative and socially liberal.

YOU GET REAL estate hustlers, beach bums, chamber of commerce types. It makes for a fascinating stew.

FLORIDA HAS world-class beaches, beautiful cotton candy sunrises and sunsets, a state park system that's won more national awards than any other.

AND OF COURSE, the world's most interesting police log.

FLORIDA'S GULF COAST is full of Midwesterners, because that's where I-75 ends. Everybody gets crammed in here, starts running around, waving their machetes at each other, arguing over whose dog pooped on whose lawn.

WE SHOULD CHANGE our name from the Sunshine State. It's misleading because most of our cities get more rain than Seattle.

WE SHOULD CALL ourselves the Most Interesting State because it's a name we could defend easily.

DO YOU WANT the news to be the same every day?

MOVE TO NEBRASKA.

WHEN I STARTED out as a reporter, I thought I had to write about military rights, drainage, fixing potholes.

I LEARNED A lot, but those weren't the stories that I wanted to tell. My bureau chief, John Cutter, taught me: "Good stories are everywhere if you just keep your eyes open."

IT WAS A revelation. There are great stories all over the place.

YOU CAN'T LIVE here and get bored. You can't. There's so much going on.

PATRICIA
HALSELL-RICHARDSON

MASTER SEAMSTRESS

I STARTED SEWING my clothes when I was 12. From there I started making clothes for other people.

I'VE ALWAYS WANTED to be a designer.

WHEN I GOT to Murphy High School in Mobile, Alabama, it was a very strange, very bad time. There were only a few African Americans there, and we were not wanted at any of the schools.

THE INSTRUCTORS of the home economics department discovered I was very talented. I was the best student they had, and I could make anything. They were just wowed.

I WENT AWAY to fashion college and came back to work with the Mobile Area Mardi Gras Association.

IT'S THE premier Black organization in Mobile. Mobile Carnival Association is the premier white organization. That's just culturally the way it is. Until there's no more white race and Black race, that's the way it'll be.

I LIKE SILK, baroque embroidery, fine fabric that doesn't stretch. I don't do a lot of sequins. Most of my work is in rhinestones and beads.

I SELECT EVERY bead and every stone. I like my things to look good in natural light.

I WANT IT to be blinging.

WHEN IT'S HAND-SEWN, it's just a much better product.

I DON'T HAVE much downtime, but when I do, I'm outta here. I'm traveling, getting ideas. New York, LA, Dubai and India are where I shop.

I LOVE MAKING trains. The first train I made was in the '70s.

PEOPLE ARE WILLING to spend a lot of money on them here. It's just Mobile culture. Mardi Gras kings and queens are the ones who pay a lot because their trains will go on display in the museum.

THEY ARE FAMILY heirlooms.

GREG ASBED AND LAURA GERMINO

FARMWORKER ORGANIZERS

GA: If not for this little piece of Florida called Immokalee, we wouldn't have domestic fruit and vegetable production between November and May in the United States.

....

GA: When you think about Florida, you think about the beaches and tourism, but it's an agricultural state.

....

LG: People may know agriculture is the second-biggest industry in the state, but what they don't realize is that Florida is the base for all of the agriculture north of here as well. Workers that harvest citrus here in the winter go up to Georgia, the Carolinas, Virginia, Missouri and Maryland in the summer.

....

GA: The culture of the farmworker community here has changed as the demographics have changed.

....

GA: It's a unique, beautiful and enduring part of America that lives in the shadows.

LG: Immokalee is a small-world town, a global crossroads. You have as many as 15 languages spoken in town ranging from English to Spanish, Creole, Hmong, Lao along with Aztec and Mayan languages.

....

LG: Throughout rural Florida and along the Gulf, there are towns like Sarasota that people see as resort towns. Yet all around Sarasota is farmwork. People who are visiting aren't aware that there is this other equally vibrant, essential and dynamic community.

....

GA: When we first started Coalition of Immokalee Farmworkers, we tried to challenge the community to think differently about what made farmworkers poor. That's when we lifted our heads up and we looked beyond the farm gates.

....

GA: We realized the retail brands have the power and are responsible for the conditions in the field.

GA: The trucks leaving the farm aren't just stopping somewhere nearby. They're taking produce to the rest of the country. They're going to these brands that everybody knows—to the Walmarts of the world, billion-dollar companies with power and a name everyone recognizes.

....

GA: We crisscrossed the country and talked to people about the fact that the food they eat comes from a place called Immokalee in Florida, where workers are denied a decent life by these massive brands.

....

LG: Organizing is not for organizing's sake. It's done in order to achieve specific transformative changes for the better.

....

GA: You can change hundreds of thousands of people's lives overnight, and that model can be expanded not just across agriculture in the U.S., but across other industries on other continents.

....

GA: When we explained the slogan "Taco Bell makes farm-

workers poor," we asked consumers to make a common cause with us to demand a new kind of food—fair food.

....

LG: What you have is the Fair Food Program today. The Gulf Coast of Florida is actually a global model for the reform of labor conditions in the supply chain worldwide.

....

GA: It's not on the scale of the civil rights movement by any means, but when people drive through these towns like LaBelle, Wauchula and especially Immokalee, it's like driving through Montgomery or across the Edmund Pettus Bridge.

....

GA: These are the places that have changed people's lives.

....

LG: You have what was one of the most regressive industries and now it's becoming one of the most progressive.

....

LG: That's something Florida should be proud of.

JESMYN WARD

WRITER

I HAVE THESE warring impulses with water.

I LOVE THE BAYOU and the swamps here on the Mississippi coast. When I was growing up, we were all too poor to have pools, so we would swim at Wolf River.

IT WAS SUCH a magical thing. All the Black families in my community of DeLisle would camp out for the weekend at the river. Like really camp in tents and cook over fires.

ON THE OTHER hand, I'm afraid of water because of hurricanes. I think I have a lot of unprocessed trauma from Katrina.

MY FAMILY HAD to go out in the middle of the storm and swim in the surge to get out of my grandmother's one-story house because we didn't want to drown in the attic.

A LOT OF *Salvage the Bones* was based on my own experience.

AFTER MY BROTHER was killed by a drunk driver, that's when I decided writing was something I wanted to pursue.

I WAS WRITING stories about home. Places I've lived in like New York City, Michigan, California didn't sing to me the way that this place did.

WHEN I WAS doing my MFA, sparse writing was lauded in class. What I was doing went against that. I felt like this place required more. A certain amount of messiness, fluidity, texture.

ONE OF THE things I'm afraid of in my work is losing touch with the place and people that inspire me. Living here, writing here, requires me to be honest.

HERE ON THE Gulf Coast, the air is a presence. There's this sense from the humidity of being wrapped up, held, supported. I tie that feeling with my community and my family here.

GROWING UP, on the Fourth of July, we would get together and eat pounds and pounds of crawfish. By the end of the day, your fingers are all cut up. They're burning. Your mouth is burning.

....

THE WOMEN IN my family make amazing seafood gumbo. But it's a very expensive, complicated dish. So that's what we get for Christmas.

....

IT'S ALWAYS BEEN an expression of love. Like, "I can't give you whatever this expensive-ass gadget is or a car or whatever, but I can give you this. This thing that I've spent all this time with and that I've made with love."

VICKI SMITH

RETIRED MERMAID PERFORMER

YOU HAD TO learn to breathe from the air hose and stay underwater for 30 minutes.

BACK IN THE '50S at Weeki Wachee Springs, all they did was give us a pair of fins and a face mask.

THESE GIRLS TODAY do their entire show without a mask. Everything they see is a blur.

THAT SPRING'S OVER 37 million years old. When you swim over the deep hole, some people get dizzy. The current down there is so strong.

YOU PULL YOURSELF down rock by rock. If you let go, it'll bang you against the cliffs and toss you around.

WE'VE SWUM WITH gators, eels, all kinds of fish. The most fun is when the manatees come up.

WHEN I WAS 17, it really was a heady experience. People were asking for my autograph. They wanted to pose with me for pictures. I still have my fan mail.

I SWAM FOR Elvis Presley in 1961.

I WAS THE mermaid that cut the ribbon to open the new million-dollar theater. My picture has been in *National Geographic*.

IT'S NEVER MADE me a rich person. But oh my gosh, I'm so, so rich in memories.

EVERYBODY WANTS TO come back and get on that air hose just one more time. No matter how old you are or how frail, it's like coming back home.

YOU'RE 17 YEARS old all over again.

THE FORMER MERMAIDS, we call ourselves the Sirens. We email each other all the time. We swim shows one weekend a month. Eight of us run a mermaid camp.

WE SHARE SOMETHING that nobody in the entire world can ever share because there's not another show like it in the entire world.

LUIS GONZALEZ

CIGAR MAKER

I SMOKE CIGARS with friends almost every day.

THEY'RE A FAMILY tradition.

MY GRANDFATHER USED to make cigars in Cuba and grow tobacco in his old-fashioned way.

I WENT TO cigar-making school in Cuba. That was around 22 years ago.

I CAME TO Tampa because a good friend of mine lived here. As soon as I arrived, I started making cigars for two different pop and mom shops in the Tampa Bay area.

A CIGAR, it's like wine. With time it's going to get better.

IN DIFFERENT PARTS of the world, cigar rollers used to handmake them by teams. The women used to pull the wrapper and the men used to put the leaves inside.

WE MAKE ABOUT 50,000 a day by machine. With a machine-made cigar, you can 100 percent control the flavor.

OUR TOBACCO COMES from different places around the world—Nicaragua, Dominican Republic or Ecuador. Every country's got different soil, different minerals. That's the flavor that the tobacco absorbs while growing.

DIFFERENT LEAVES have different flavors. The flavor also depends on how many leaves you put inside the cigar, plus the wrapper.

CIGARS THAT spend more time in the aging room are a little stronger. When it's dark brown, or sometimes black, that's a full-bodied cigar.

CIGAR ROLLERS from Spain came to Cuba, then to Tampa about a hundred years ago, and now Tampa is the capital of the cigar.

IT'S BEAUTIFUL that we have kept the tradition here for so long.

CHRIS WIRT

WILDLIFE REMOVAL SPECIALIST

I'VE CAUGHT WILD animals my whole life.

JUVENILE BOBCATS, they're pretty strong.

YOU CAN FEEL the crushing pressure of their jaws when they bite, whether or not they leave a mark.

I'VE BEEN BIT multiple times by nonvenomous snakes too.

I WAS A FIREMAN for more than 20 years. I was always helping people catch animals. When I retired, I decided to start my own business in Tampa.

THE BIGGEST THING is self-study. Do your own research. Just go out in the woods and watch the animals.

RATS, SQUIRRELS, flying squirrels, raccoons, possums. Those are the most common ones we see. Oh and armadillos.

WE'VE CAUGHT A monkey in an attic. Caught a capybara, which is about a 135-pound rodent.

WE CATCH TEGUS in Riverview. It's basically an armored lizard.

ANY ANIMAL that's injured we take to a vet to decide if it has to be euthanized or if it can go to rehab.

WE HAVE reinforced gloves to protect against bites. We have catch poles of different sizes depending on how far away we have to stay.

WHEN WE'RE AT someone's home, we educate them on the animal in their attic.

NOT ONLY ARE we helping people, we're also helping animals so that someone doesn't get scared and just kill them.

FROM THE TIME you're young, you're taught that snakes are the devil, evil, they'll kill you.

SNAKES actually have proteins in their venom used in medications for leukemia, breast cancer, hemophilia.

ONE VENOMOUS SNAKE can save thousands of lives.

DUANE NUTTER

CHEF

GROWING UP IN Morgan City, Louisiana, I was fascinated with what was happening in the kitchen. That's where family always congregated around a good conversation.

I WAS LIKE, "What's going on in there?"

ONE TIME WHEN I was little I wondered what the noise was in a pot on the stove.

I GOT A steam burn on my chest when I looked in and saw blue crabs jumping around.

I'VE BEEN ALL over. I went to cooking school in Seattle. I worked in Florida at the Ritz-Carlton. I was a Five Diamond chef in Louisville at the Seelbach Hilton. I was a spokesperson for the National Peanut Board and traveled the country in a car.

I ALSO STARTED dibble-dabbling in comedy. When I was a morning sous-chef, I would go around telling jokes in the clubs at night.

I HAD A NOTEBOOK for prep work in the kitchen and a book to write down anything funny that happened around me.

ALL OF THAT traveling inspires my food, but it's always rooted in where I'm from—the Gulf Coast.

PEOPLE HERE KNOW how to cook for themselves better than anywhere.

MY BUSINESS PARTNER, Reggie Washington, is from here. Our restaurant's name, Southern National, came from how people labeled my food at One Flew South in the Atlanta airport.

MOBILE IS a cool place that people don't want you to know exists.

IT'S ON THE cusp of changing over. There's a tug of war between the old guard and the new.

IT'S ONE OF the reasons I came here. To move this place forward.

IT'S GOT THE makings of somewhere that can be, like, "whoa."

STORIES

Essays and selected writing from
noted Gulf Coast voices

SALTWATER IN THE WOUND

Written by **SCOTT HOCKER** | **SHIP ISLAND HAD A WOUND.**
A saltwater gash formed in 1969. The
first time I visited the barrier island, 11 or so miles off the coast of
Gulfport, Mississippi, was June 7, 2015. By then, 45 years had passed
since Hurricane Camille bifurcated Ship Island into West Ship Island
and East Ship Island and almost 10 years since Hurricane Katrina
exacerbated the laceration.

I had been living in New Orleans for only six months; Ship Island had
been in the Gulf of Mexico far longer. The sliver of an island was formed
5,000 years earlier, a spring chicken in geological terms. Its wound, then,
was fresh. As was mine. This was my first summer in the Deep South, the
heat torpid, and my eight-year partnership was fissuring. I tried to plaster
the clefts as they formed, when I bothered to acknowledge them. Brandon
and I had always been good at roaming. "Adventure Times" we called it.
We were better afield than we were at home. The drip and swelter of late
spring in New Orleans begged for a jaunt, so the two of us sought open
water. Someone, somewhere in a conversation one day had mentioned
Ship Island. They noted the water was clear and blue. Not like the
brownish murk of the waters along Mississippi's mainland coast.

I am sitting in a camping chair on Waveland Beach, located about a third
of the way between the western and eastern edges of Mississippi's 44 miles
of shoreline. It is late August 2020, five years after my debut summer in the
Deep South, and a pandemic rages. My friend Courtney and I drive the
lazy hour from New Orleans for an easy beachside respite after months
of isolation. We drive the more scenic of the two main roads, Highway 90.
It ambles past Bayou Sauvage, over the Rigolets strait and the Pearl River,
and into Mississippi. Sometimes we use Interstate 10. That route is more
expeditious. Whichever highway we use, I see unfamiliar topography
and flora. This is a latitude and a near-country away from the open-water

environs I know best, the Pacific Ocean where it crashes into Northern California. There, in the region where I was raised, the trees—tanoaks and redwoods and the Pacific madrone—cede in a steep, craggy instant to the frothy brawl of the cracking surf. My dad is a scuba diver. The ocean is what he does, so it is what our family did, too. In coastal Mississippi, I still lack the familiarity, the language, to name what is around me. Each time I visit Waveland, or Bay Saint Louis up the road, or Pass Christian across Bay Saint Louis' namesake estuary, I gape and fumble and wonder WWJD: What Would Jesmyn Do? Jesmyn Ward, the bard of this patch of Mississippi. Jesmyn Ward, whose home is inland a few miles to the northeast, in DeLisle. She knows this place, its marsh grass, its swamp myrtle, its saw palmetto, knows her region's markers and their names. I want to survey it the way she does.

The ferry to Ship Island puttered across the Gulf for 90 slow minutes. Brandon and I gathered our tote bags snug with blankets and sunscreen and rum punch and wine [and, yes, water] and disembarked at West Ship Island. We shuffled past Fort Massachusetts, a Civil War stronghold, in our flip-flops, Brandon ahead of me, down a long, angling boardwalk. Tall grass stretched high and wide on both sides. I later learned its name: shoal grass. At the boardwalk's end, there was a snack bar and an outfitter where visitors could rent bright blue umbrellas and lounge chairs. Brandon and I decided the Gulf's waters would be our reprieve when the sun's scorch became unbearable. We baked and drank until the temperature turned insistent. Then we glided across the torrid white sand and threw ourselves into the gentle surf. The quiet green-blue water was nothing like the raucous breakers of my youth. In Northern California, I avoided the water. It was frigid. At Ship Island, the Gulf's ease was an invitation, one Brandon and I accepted a handful of times in 2015 and 2016 during the island's annual operating season from March to October. A recurring reset for two men trying to find their way back to each other. And failing.

It is September 6, 2016. I am unable, again, to use my words with Brandon. They crumble in my mouth. I enlist my default maneuver: active silence. I am in pain so I punish him by escaping New Orleans for the beachfront in Bay Saint Louis. It is a double betrayal: lock him out by muting myself; rove without him, abandoning him when I know he also wants a beach getaway. I park and tromp and stew. A collection of stones, some large as

footballs, lines this stretch of the shore near the Washington Street Pier. My love for Brandon remains firm, but the common ground between us slips. Erosion is a slow muck. Second to hour, sameness. Five thousand years, though, can fashion a barrier island; a decade can bind two men. Then each is rended asunder in a cataclysmic flash.

I have been visiting Waveland Beach with Courtney every weekend for five weeks by this point in October 2020. It is two years since Brandon left our relationship, one year since he moved to the other side of the United States. I have not visited Ship Island in four years. Since then, the island has been conjoined into a reunited mass when, in 2019, millions of cubic yards of sand were pumped to fill the gap created by Camille and Katrina. So it goes. So it will happen again. Jesmyn has made me see, and I have begun naming the world around me: Those spiky trees plopped in clusters along Waveland Beach are *Washingtonia robusta*, Mexican fan palms. Those wispy tendrils are sea oats, native *Uniola paniculata L.*, their panicles turning from green to straw-gold as the summer wanes. The shallows of Waveland Beach extend far into the Gulf, or at least farther than I am used to. The locals around us have moved their lawn chairs into the water itself and speared their umbrellas into the nearshore zone. Courtney, the only Black person in sight, is letting the water wash away, for a spell, her trepidation about being Black in the United States and being Black on this here stretch along the southernmost edge of the Deep South. My dog, Logan, is learning to like open water, provided open water lets his paws maintain contact with sturdy earth. These shallows are a balm, regular life held in bathwater abeyance. Impermanence is permanent here on the Mississippi Gulf Coast. Wounds erupt; wounds mend.

SCOTT HOCKER is a writer, problem-solver-for-hire and the former editor in chief of *Tasting Table* and Liquor.com. He is from the San Francisco Bay Area and has lived all over the United States but is now rooted in New Orleans. He is often enveloped by water, ideally in an ocean or a sea or lake but sometimes just his bathtub.

HOW THE SAUCE IS MADE

Written by **LADEE HUBBARD** | **SIX MILES SOUTH** of New Iberia, Louisiana, sits Avery Island, best known as the home of Tabasco Pepper Sauce. Like the pepper in the famous sauce's name, the designation "island" is somewhat of a misnomer. Surrounded by bayous, salt marshes and swamps, Avery Island is actually 2,200 acres of lush semitropical marshland set atop an 8-mile-deep natural salt dome. It was here that, in 1868, Edmund McIlhenny, a former New Orleans banker left destitute by the Civil War, began manufacturing Tabasco, making it one of the oldest sauce brands in the country. Initially sold locally in cologne bottles, Tabasco has since grown to become a global commodity, currently available in 192 countries and so ubiquitous that, for many people, the brand's name is synonymous with hot sauce itself.

I first became aware of Avery Island while doing research for a novel. Set in 1914, the story centers around the experiences of a man who invents a meat sauce that like Tabasco, becomes an extremely popular national brand. One of the things I wanted to explore when I wrote the book was how the increased circulation and distribution of commodities in the early 20th century affected ideas about identity, community and local culture. Tabasco, which is often associated with Louisiana identity and which was emerging as a global brand during the same period in which my novel is set, became a focal point of a broader inquiry into the intersecting symbolism of food as both a commodity and a source of sustenance.

Incredibly, the Tabasco company is still family-owned and continues to operate out of Avery Island, and so a visit offered the opportunity to witness firsthand how the sauce is made. The on-site museum documents the story of how McIlhenny, after years of experimentation, determined that aging his sauce greatly improved its specific taste. His method of production involved grinding the chiles into a mash, mixing it with the island's natural rock salt and aging it in jars for 30 days. Vinegar was then added, and the sauce was pickled for another month.

A tour of the factory demonstrated how this original process continues to inform production today. The period of fermentation has been extended from its initial two months to an average of three years, and in order to keep up with demand, the chiles are now farmed in various locations in Latin America. But all of the seeds still originate from Avery Island, and once the chiles are cultivated overseas, they are sent back to be mixed with salt [mined from underneath the dome] and aged in large oak barrels. The company has been able to continue to operate out of its original location, all while manufacturing up to 750,000 bottles of sauce per day.

Preservation—in terms of Tabasco's production methods, the use of traditional, local ingredients and the brand's association with a particular place—was a theme that resonated in other aspects of the island as well, becoming a concrete expression of the McIlhenny family's influence there. Just across the road from the Tabasco facility is Jungle Gardens, a 170-acre botanical garden and wildlife sanctuary that stretches along the Bayou Petite Anse and was established by Ned McIlhenny, son of Tabasco's founder. Within Jungle Gardens is Bird City, one of the oldest bird sanctuaries in the United States, often credited with having saved the snowy white egret from extinction in the 1920s, when the population was threatened because of the overuse of their feathers in the making of ladies' hats. Today, thousands of egrets can be seen on the island as well as numerous other species of animals, including white-tailed deer, otters, muskrats, alligators and Louisiana black bear.

All of this emphasis on preservation seemed fitting of a place that was literally made of salt. It occurred to me that the only two other ingredients of Tabasco—chile and vinegar—are, of course, preservatives themselves. In a slight deviation from the focus of my novel, I began to consider how the cultural histories of all of these ingredients, and in particular the chiles, told a much broader story, through the central role they have long played in the circulation of food products themselves.

Capsaicin, the unique chemical substance that makes chiles "hot," is like salt and vinegar, a powerful antimicrobial. Chile sauce not only makes food taste better, but also helps keep good food from going bad—a fact that has contributed greatly to hot sauce's appeal, in various incarnations, throughout the world.

All of these incarnations are traceable to the Americas. One of the world's earliest cultivated crops, the chile is indigenous to the Americas and, like the tomato, potato and corn, made its way into the cuisines of Europe, Asia and Africa through various trade routes at the service of slavery, colonialism and global commerce. Given the chile's current associations with a wide variety of cuisines, the specificity of its origins in Mesoamerica is frequently obscured by its identification as a pepper—a misnomer attributed to a confused Columbus, who associated it with peppercorn because of its comparable "spicy taste."

Long before Columbus' arrival, Native Mesoamericans recognized the chile's usefulness as medicine. Its association with U.S. Southern and African American cuisine is in part an expression of cultural affinity, as prior to its introduction in Africa by the Portuguese, the people of West and Central Africa used strong spices not only to flavor foods but to treat various ailments. This affinity for the spicy was in part transferred to the chile during the slave trade, when some slave owners actively encouraged the consumption of chiles, based on their own beliefs that they kept slaves healthy.

In Louisiana, the chile's broader consumption in the mid-19th century is often associated with the advocacy of a man named Maunsel White, a sugar planter who firmly believed that chiles had kept his slaves from getting sick during a cholera outbreak. White created several sauces from different chiles, including the distinctive tabasco variety he introduced almost 20 years before McIlhenny began bottling his. White sold his sauces to oyster bars while actively promoting their consumption among the white slaveholding aristocracy, often distributing bottles as gifts to his friends, including Andrew Jackson.

By the mid-19th century, homemade pepper sauces were popular throughout Louisiana, crafted from recipes that utilized a wide variety of supplemental ingredients and modes of preparation. Most of these recipes featured the more commonly accessible cayenne pepper, however, and so McIlhenny's product, heralding the use of the distinctive tabasco, was initially a way to distinguish itself in an already crowded field.

Thus, the product most associated with regional identity was originally an eccentric variant. It now stands as one of the most iconic emblems of Louisiana culture, despite being named for a region of Mexico that Edmund McIlhenny never even visited. According to legend, McIlhenny received the original, unidentified seeds as a gift from a Confederate soldier who had recently visited Mexico; he planted them on Avery Island, at the time a sugar plantation owned by his wife's family. He then forgot about them until he returned following the Civil War and found the chiles, the basis of the family fortune, growing wild.

The specifics of this story are, like many official narratives of history, disputed. It gives no account of White's previous experiments with Tabasco or of the contributions of both Indigenous Americans and African Americans to the knowledge of and efforts to cultivate the chile more broadly. And yet it is a fascinating story, because of the ways it both stubbornly deflects and embodies its own contradictions about identity, culture and the inextricable intersection between the global and the local. Which in turn makes Tabasco—as a highly refined preservative, source of sustenance and carefully curated brand—a fitting emblem for Louisiana itself.

LADEE HUBBARD is the author of *The Rib King* and *The Talented Ribkins*, which received the 2018 Ernest J. Gaines Award for Literary Excellence. Born in Massachusetts and raised in the U.S. Virgin Islands and Florida, she currently lives in New Orleans with her husband and three children.

ONE ACRE

Written by **JOY WILLIAMS**

I HAD AN ACRE IN FLORIDA, on a lagoon close by the Gulf of Mexico.

I am admittedly putting this first line up against Isak Dinesen's famous oneiric one: *I had a farm in Africa, at the foot of the Ngong Hills.* When Dinesen first came to Africa she confessed that she could not "live without getting a fine specimen of each single kind of African game." For her the hunt was an eroticized image of desire, "a love affair," wherein the "shot ... was in reality a declaration of love." She must have blushed to read this drivel later, for after ten years she found hunting "an unreasonable thing, indeed in itself ugly and vulgar, for the sake of a few hours enjoyment to put out a life that belonged in the great landscape and had grown up on it." One could say her thinking had evolved, that she had become more conscientious. Still, when she was about to leave her beloved farm [her house, empty of furniture, was admirably "clean like a skull"], she planned to shoot her dogs and horses, dissuaded from doing so only by the pleas of her friends. The animals belonged to her, as had the land, which she ceased to own only when it became owned by another, and subject to that person's whims and policies. Of course it became hers again through writing about it, preserving it in *Out of Africa.* Once again, Art, reflective poesy, saves landscape.

I had an acre in Florida ... This bodes no drama. For what wonders could a single acre hold, what meaning or relevance? Although the word "Florida" is oneiric, too, and thus its own metaphor. It is an occasional place, a palmed and pleasant stage for transients. To hold fast to an acre in that vast state is almost neurotic. An acre is both too much and not enough. Its value lies in its divisibility, in how many building lots are permitted by law. Four, certainly.

I once saw a white heron in a tumbled landscape on the sprawling outskirts of Naples, a city that crowds against the Big Cypress National Preserve and Everglades National Park. The heron seemed to be beating its head against a tree knocked down by bulldozers to widen a road. Water still lay along the palmetto-dotted earth, but pipes would soon carry it away and dry the land for town houses and golf courses. Cars sped past. The heron, white as a robed angel must surely be, was beating his head against the tree. He was lost to himself, deranged, in his ruined and lost landscape.

I have seen all manner of beautiful waterbirds struck down by cars. I used to take them home and bury them between the mangroves and the live oaks on my lagoon. But of course it was not *my* lagoon, this body of water only a mile and a half long. To the north it cedes to a private road that gives access to the Sanderling Club, where the exceptionally wealthy enjoy their Gulf views. To the south it vanishes beneath the parking lot for a public beach. This is on Siesta Key, a crowded eight-mile-long island off Sarasota that is joined to the mainland by two bridges, one four lanes, the other two. The lagoon is named Heron; the beach, Tuttle. Yes, the turtles still come to nest, and the volunteers who stake and guard the nests are grateful— they practically weep with gratitude—when the condo dwellers keep their lights out during the hatching weeks so as not to confuse the infant turtles in their night search for the softly luminous sea. But usually the condo dwellers don't keep their lights out. They might accommodate the request were they there, but they are seldom there. The lights are controlled by timers and burn bright and long. The condos are investments, mostly, not homes. Like the lands they've consumed, they're cold commodities. When land is developed, it ceases being land. It becomes covered, sealed, its own grave.

Ecosystems are something large to be saved, if at all, by the government at great expense and set aside to be enjoyed by all of us in some recreational or contemplative fashion. An individual doesn't think of himself as owning an ecosystem. The responsibility! Too much. Besides, there's something about the word that denotes the impossibility of ownership. *Land*, on the other hand, is like a car or a house; it has economic currency. Aldo Leopold defined land as *a fountain of energy flowing through a circuit of soils, plants, and animals*; it was synonymous with ecosystem, and he argued that we all have an obligation to protect and preserve it. It was over fifty years ago that Leopold wrote his elegantly reasoned essay "The Land Ethic," but it has had about as much effect on the American conscience as a snowflake. Seven thousand acres are lost to development each day in this country. Ecosystem becomes land becomes parcel.

On Siesta Key, "open space" [of which there is now none], when bought by the county years ago, is being utilized as beach parking or tennis courts. "Raw" land no longer exists, though a few lots are still available, some with very nice trees, most of which will have to go [unfortunately] in order to accommodate the house that will be built on what is now considered a "site." We hardly can get all ecosystem emotional over a site. A banyan tree will most assuredly have to go because it is in its nature to grow extravagantly and demand a great deal of space. Trees, of course, cannot *demand* anything. As with the wild animals who have certain requirements or preferences—a clutter and cover, long natural hours of friendly concealing dark—anything they *need* can be ignored or removed right along with them.

In 1969, I bought Lots 27, 28, and 29 on Midnight Pass Road, a two-lane road that ended when the key did. There was a small cypress house, no beauty, and an even smaller cypress cottage. They were single-story affairs with flat roofs, built on poured slabs. The lots together cost $24,000. In 1972, I bought Lots 30 and 31 for $12,000. Lagoon land wasn't all that desirable. There was no access to open water. Bay land was more valuable, and even then Gulf front was only for the wealthy. Beachfront is invaluable because no one can build on the sea; the view is "protected." I could hear the Gulf on my small acre; it was, in fact, only several hundred feet away, concealed by a scrim of mangroves. The houses that were to be built over there were grand but still never quite exceeded the height of the mangroves. I did not see my lagoon neighbors for my trees, my tangled careless land, though as the years passed I put up sections of wooden fence, for my neighbors changed, then changed again, and their little cypress houses were torn down in a twinkling, the "extra" lots sold. I put a wooden fence up along the road eventually. It weathered prettily but would shudder on its posts from a flung beer bottle. Sections of it were periodically demolished by errant cars. I don't believe I ever rushed sympathetically to the befuddled driver's aid. No one actually died, but they did go on, those crashes. Streetlights went up at fifty-foot intervals on the dark and curvy road. The bay side got the lights, the lagoon side got the bicycle path. Homeowners were responsible for keeping the "path" tidy, and I appeared out there dutifully with broom and rake, pushing away the small oak leaves from the trees that towered overhead, disclosing all that efficient concrete for the benefit of increasing streams of walkers and joggers. Bicyclists preferred to use the road. Any stubborn palmetto that fanned outward or seeded palm that once graced the strip of land outside my rickety wall would be snipped back by a supernumerary, doing his/her part for the

public way. The bottles, cans, and wee chip bags were left for me to reap. As owner of Lots 27, 28, 29, 30, and 31, I had 370 feet of path to maintain. I became aware, outside my fence, of the well-known Florida light, a sort of blandly insistent *urban* light—feathery and bemused and resigned. Cars sped past. Large houses were being constructed on the bay, estates on half an acre with elaborate wrought-iron fences and electric gates. Palmetto scrub had given way to lawns. Trees existed as dramatically trimmed accents, all dead wood removed. Trees not deemed perfectly sound by landscape professionals were felled; the palms favored were "specimen" ones. Dead animals and birds appeared more and more frequently on the road. Cars sped past.

Behind my wobbly fence, I pottered about. The houses were built in the forties, and the land had the typical homesteaded accoutrements of that time—a few citrus trees, some oleander and hibiscus for color, a plot cleared for a few vegetables and Shasta daisies, a fig left to flourish for shade, and live oaks left to grow around the edges. The ghastly malleucas were available in nurseries then and were often planted in rows as a hedge. The man I bought the land from was a retired botanist, and he had planted avocado and lychee nut trees too, as well as a grove of giant bamboo from which he liked to make vases and bowls and various trinkets. There was bougainvillea, azalea, gardenia, powder puff and firecracker plant, crotons, wild lilies, sea grape, and several orchid trees. Of the palms there was a royal, sabal, many cabbage, pineapple, sago—queen and king—reclinata, fishtail, sentry, traveler's, and queen. There were cypresses, jacaranda, and two banyan trees. There was even a tiny lawn with small cement squares to place the lawn chairs on. The mangroves in this spot had been cut back for a view of the idly flowing tea-colored lagoon. Elsewhere they grew—the red and the black—in the manner each found lovely, in hoops and stands, creating bowers and thickets and mazes of rocking water and dappling light.

This was my acre in Florida. Visitors ventured that it looked as though it would require an awful lot of maintenance, though they admired my prescience in buying the extra lots, which would surely be worth something someday. The house had a certain "rustic charm," but most people didn't find the un-air-conditioned, un-dehumidified air all that wholesome and wondered why I kept the place so damn dark, for there were colored floods widely available that would dramatize the "plantings." I could bounce more lights off the water, you could hardly even tell there was water out there, and what was the sense of hiding that? And despite the extraordinary variety, my land seemed unkempt. There were vines and Brazilian pepper and carrotwood, there were fire-ant mounds, rats surely lived in the fronds of the untrimmed palms. My acre looked a little hesitant, small and vulnerable, *young*. Even the banyan tree was relatively young. It had put down a few aerials but then stopped for a good decade as if it were thinking ... *What's the use. I'm straddling Lots 29 & 30 and I'm not known as an accommodating tree. When the land gets sold, I'll be sold, too and will fall in screaming suttee* ... Or sentiments of that sort.

As for the birds and animals, well, people didn't want raccoons and opossums and armadillos, and their cats would eat the baby rabbits. Too disgusting, but that's just the way nature *was*. And although I had cardinals and towhees and thrashers and mockingbirds and doves and woodpeckers, they did, too; as a matter of fact their cardinals were nesting in a place where they could actually see them, right near the front door, and that was getting to be quite the nuisance. As for the herons, you found them everywhere, even atop the dumpsters behind the 7-Eleven. Such beggars. You had to chase them away from your bait bucket when you were fishing from the beach. Did I fish in the lagoon? There were snapper in there, redfish, maybe even snook. I could get the mullet with nets. Why didn't I fish?

The years flowed past. Some of the properties on the lagoon fell to pure speculation. Mangroves were pruned like any hedging material; in some cases, decks were built over them, causing them to die, though they remained ghostily rooted. Landowners on the Gulf did not molest their mangrove. The lagoon to them was the equivalent of a back alley. Why would they want to regard the increasing myriad of houses huddled there? I traveled, I rented the place out, I returned. There were freezes, we were grazed by hurricanes. An immense mahoe hibiscus died back in a cold snap, and two years later a tall, slender, smooth-barked tree it had been concealing began producing hundreds of the pinkest, sweetest, juiciest grapefruit I have ever tasted. The water oaks that had reached their twenty-year limit rotted and fell. There were lovely woodpeckers. All through the winter in the nights the chuck-will's-widows would call.

That would drive me nuts, several of my acquaintants remarked.

The sound of construction was almost constant, but no one appeared to be actually living in the remodeled, enlarged, upgraded properties around me. I had cut out sections of my side fences to allow oak limbs to grow in their tortured specific manner, but my neighbor's yardmen would eventually be instructed to lop them off at the property line. This was, of course, the owner's right. There was the sound of trimmers, leaf blowers, pool pumps, pressure cleaners; the smell of chemicals from pest and lawn services. Maintenance maintenance maintenance. Then the county began cutting back the live oak limbs that extended over the bicycle path, even though one would have to be an idiot on a pogo stick to bump into one. Sliced sure as bread, the limbs, one at least five feet in diameter and green with resurrection fern and air plants, were cut back to the fence line.

It was then I decided to build the wall.

The year was 1990. The wall was of cement block with deep footers, and it ran the entire length of the property except for a twelve-foot opening, which was gated in cedar. It cost about $10,000, and two men did it in two months. The wall was ten feet high. It was not stuccoed. I thought it was splendid. I didn't know many people in the neighborhood by then, but word got back to me that some did not find it attractive. What did I have back there, a prison? To me, it was the people speeding past the baby Tajs on the animal-corpse-littered road who had become imprisoned. Inside was land—a mysterious, messy fountain of energy; outside was something else—not land in any meaningful sense but a diced bright salad of colorful real estate, pods of investment, its value now shrilly, sterilely economic.

Behind the wall was an Edenic acre, still known to the tax collector as Lots 27, 28, 29, 30, and 31. Untransformed by me, who was neither gardener nor crafty ecological restorer, the land had found its own rich dynamic. Behind the wall were neither grounds nor yard nor garden, nor park, nor even false jungle, but a functioning wild landscape that became more remarkable each year. Of course there was the humble house and even humbler cottage, which appeared less and less important to me in the larger order of things. They were shelters, pleasant enough but primarily places from which to look *out* at the beauty of a world to which I was irrelevant except for my role of preserving it, a world I could be integrated with only to the extent of my not harming it. The wildlife could hardly know that their world in that place existed only because I, rather than another, *owned it*. I knew, though, and the irrationality of the arrangement, the premise, angered me and made me feel powerless, for I did not feel that the land was mine at all but rather belonged to something larger that was being threatened by something absurdly small, the ill works and delusions of—as William Burroughs liked to say—*homo sap.*

Although the wall did not receive social approbation, its approval from an ecological point of view was resounding. The banyan, as though reassured by the audacious wall, flung down dozens of aerial roots. The understory flourished; the oaks soared, creating a great grave canopy. Plantings that had seemed tentative when I had bought them from botanical gardens years before took hold. The leaves and bark crumble built up, the ferns spread. It was odd. I fancied that I had made an inside for the outside to be safe in. From within, the wall vanished; green growth pressed against it, staining it naturally brown and green and black. It muffled the sound and heat of the road. Inside was cool and dappled, hymned with birdsong. There were owls and wood ducks. An osprey roosted each night in a casuarina that leaned out over the lagoon, a tree of no good reputation and half-dead, but the osprey deeply favored it, folding himself into it invisibly in a few seconds each nightfall. A pair of yellow-crowned night herons nested in a slash pine in the center of Lot 30. Large birds with a large hidden nest, their young—each year three!—not hasty in their departure. A single acre was able to nurture so many lives, including mine. Its existence gave me great happiness.

And yet it was all an illusion too, a shadow box, for when I opened the gates or canoed the lagoon, I saw an utterly different world. This was a world that had fallen only in part to consortiums of developers; it had fallen mostly plat by plat to individuals, who, paradoxically, were quite conformist in their attitude toward land, or rather the scraped scaffolding upon which their real property was built. They lived in penury of a very special sort, but that was only my opinion. In *their* opinion they were living in perfect accord with the values of the time, successfully and cleverly, taking advantage of their advantages. Their attitudes were perfectly acceptable; they were not behaving unwisely or without foresight. They had maximized profits, and if little of nature had been preserved in the arrangement, well, nature was an adornment not to everyone's taste, a matter really of personal tolerance and sympathy. Besides, Nature was not far away, supported by everyone's tax dollars and preserved in state and federal parks. And one could show one's appreciation for these places by visiting them at any time. Public lands can be projected as having as many recreational, aesthetic, or environmental benefits as can be devised for them, but private land, on this skinny Florida key and almost everywhere in this country, is considered too economically valuable to be conserved. Despoliation of land in its many, many guises is the custom of the country.

Privately, one by one, the landowner makes decisions that render land, in any other than financial terms, moot. Land is something to be "built out."

In contrast to its surrounds, my acre appeared an evasion of reality, a construct, a moment poised before an inevitable after. How lovely it was, how fortunate I was. Each day my heart recognized its great worth. It was invaluable to me. The moment came when I had to sell it.

Leopold speaks of the necessity of developing an ecological conscience, of having an awareness of land in a philosophical rather than an economic sense. His articulation of our ethical obligations to the land is considered by many to be quite admirable. We celebrated the fiftieth anniversary of this articulation [if not its implementation] in 1999. A pretty thought, high-minded. And yet when one has to *move on* [if not exactly in the final sense] one is expected to be sensible, realistic, even canny, about property. I was not in the comfortable kind of financial situation where I could deed my land to a conservation group or land trust. Even if I could have, it would probably have been sold to protect more considerable sanctuary acreage elsewhere, for it was a mere acre in a pricey neighborhood, not contiguous with additional habitat land, though the lagoon did provide a natural larger dimension. I had been developing an ecological conscience for thirty years, and I could continue to develop it still certainly, become a good steward somewhere else, because once I had decided to sell, this particular piece of land and all the creatures that found it to be a perfect earthly home would be subject to erasure in any meaningful ecological sense, and this would not be considered by society to be selfish, cruel, or irresponsible.

A SINGLE ACRE WAS ABLE TO NURTURE SO MANY LIVES, INCLUDING MINE. ITS EXISTENCE GAVE ME GREAT HAPPINESS.

"Wow, it's great back here," the realtor said. "I often wondered what the heck was going on back here. I'm looking forward to showing this place."

I told him I wanted to sell the land as a single piece, with deed restrictions, these being that the land could never be subdivided; that the buildings be restricted to one house and cottage taking up no more land than the originals; and that the southern half of the property be left in its natural state as wildlife habitat.

"Nobody wants to be told what they can do with their land," he told me, frowning. "I'll mention your wishes, but you'll have to accept a significant reduction in price with those kinds of restrictions. When we get an offer you and the buyer can negotiate the wording of the agreement. I'm sure the type of person who would be attracted to this property wouldn't want to tear it all apart."

"Really," I said, "you don't think?"

I went through a number of realtors.

With a lawyer I drew up a simple and enforceable document that the realtors found so unnerving that they wouldn't show it right away to interested parties, preferring word wobble and expressions of goodwill. There were many people who *loved* the land, who *loved* nature, but would never buy anything that was in essence not free and clear. Or they had no problem with the restrictions *personally*, but when they had to sell [and Heaven forbid that they would right away of course] they could not impose such coercive restraints on others. The speculators and builders had been dismissed from the beginning. These were people of a more maverick bent, *caring* people who loved Florida, loved the key—wasn't it a shame there was so much development, so much change. When they saw the humble document they said 1] who does she think she *is*? 2] she's crazy, 3] she'll never sell it. Over the months the realtors took on a counseling manner with me as though I needed guidance through this dark stubborn wood of my own making, as though I needed to be talked down from my irrational fanciful resolve. They could sell the land for $200,000 more if I dropped the restrictions. My acre could be destroyed naturally; a hurricane could level everything, and the creatures, the birds, would have to go somewhere else anyway. With the money I'd make marketing it smartly, I could buy a hundred acres, maybe more, east of the interstate. There was a lot of pretty ranchland over there. I could conserve that. A lot of pressure would be on that land in a few years; I could do more by saving that. Sell and don't look back! That's what people did. You can't look back.

I'm not looking back, I said.

And I wasn't.

I was looking ahead, seeing the land behind the wall still existent, still supporting its nests and burrows—a living whole. I was leaving it—soon I would no longer be personally experiencing its loveliness—but I would not abandon it, I would despise myself if I did. If I were to be party to a normal real estate transaction, I would be dooming it, I would be—and this is not at all exaggerated—signing a warrant for its death. [Perhaps the owners of the four new houses that could—and would, most likely—be built would have the kindness to put out some birdseed.] I wanted more than money for my land, more than the mere memory of it, the luxury of conserving it falsely and sentimentally through lyrical recall. I wanted it to *be*.

It took eight months to find the right buyer. Leopold's "philosophers" were in short supply in the world of Florida real estate. But the ideal new owners eventually appeared, and they had no problem with the contract between themselves and the land. I had changed no hearts or minds by my attitude or actions; I had simply found—or my baffled but determined realtors had—people of my persuasion, people who had a land ethic, too. Their duties as stewards were not onerous to them. They did not consider the additional legal documents they were obliged to sign an insult to their personal freedom. They were aware that the principle was hardly radical. An aunt had done a similar thing in New England, preserving forty acres of meadow and woodland by conservation easement. They had friends in California who had similarly sold and conserved by deed four hundred acres of high desert. And here was this enchanted acre.

It had been accomplished. I had persisted. I was well pleased with myself. Selfishly I had affected the land beyond my tenure. I had gotten my way.

And with all of this, I am still allowed to miss it so.

JOY WILLIAMS is the author of novels, collections of short stories and *Ill Nature*, a book of essays that was a finalist for the National Book Critics Circle Award. Her novel *The Quick and the Dead* was a runner-up for the Pulitzer Prize in 2001. She also wrote *The Florida Keys: A History and Guide*, now in its 10th edition. Williams lives in Tucson, Arizona, and Key West, Florida. This essay was originally pulished in the February 2001 issue of *Harper's Magazine*.

THEORIES OF TIME AND SPACE

Written by **NATASHA TRETHEWEY**

You can get there from here, though
there's no going home.

Everywhere you go will be somewhere
you've never been. Try this:

head south on Mississippi 49, one—
by—one mile markers ticking off

another minute of your life. Follow this
to its natural conclusion—dead end

at the coast, the pier at Gulfport where
riggings of shrimp boats are loose stitches

in a sky threatening rain. Cross over
the man-made beach, 26 miles of sand

dumped on a mangrove swamp—buried
terrain of the past. Bring only

what you must carry—tome of memory
its random blank pages. On the dock

where you board the boat for Ship Island,
someone will take your picture:

the photograph—who you were—
will be waiting when you return

NATASHA TRETHEWEY served two terms as the 19th poet laureate of the United States (2012–2014), while also serving as the poet laureate of the state of Mississippi (2012–2016). She is the author of *The New York Times* bestseller *Memorial Drive: A Daughter's Memoir, Beyond Katrina: A Meditation on the Mississippi Gulf Coast* and five collections of poetry, including *Native Guard*, for which she was awarded the Pulitzer Prize.

DIRECTORY
& INDEX

DIRECTORY

SEAFOOD SPOTS

83 West *Cedar Key, FL*

Billy's Seafood *Bon Secour, AL*

Bluegill Restaurant *Spanish Fort, AL*

Bon Creole Lunch Counter *New Iberia, LA*

Bozo's Seafood Market *Pascagoula, MS*

Brocato's Sandwich Shop *Tampa, FL*

Callaghan's Irish Social Club *Mobile, AL*

Casamento's *New Orleans, LA*

Columbia Restaurant *Ybor City, FL*

Delcambre Seafood *Delcambre, LA*

Fisher's *Orange Beach, AL*

French Hermit Oyster Co. *Deer Island, MS*

Hole in the Wall *Apalachicola, FL*

Killer Seafood *Mexico Beach, FL*

Lorene's Fish House *St. Petersburg, FL*

Lynn's Quality Oysters *Eastpoint, FL*

Manci's Antique Club *Daphne, AL*

Mermaid Tavern *Tampa, FL*

Mineral Springs Seafood *Panacea, FL*

Mosquito Supper Club *New Orleans, LA*

Mr. Shrimp *New Orleans, LA*

Murder Point Oysters *Bayou La Batre, AL*

Ouzts' Too Oyster Bar *Crawfordville, FL*

Owen's Fish Camp *Sarasota, FL*

Pascal's Manale *New Orleans, LA*

The Pink Elephant *Boca Grande, FL*

Pêche *New Orleans, LA*

Sandbar Restaurant *Anna Maria Island, FL*

Shelly's Seafood Market *Homosassa, FL*

Siesta Key Oyster Bar *Siesta Key, FL*

Southern National *Mobile, AL*

Star Fish Company Market *Cortez, FL*

The Station Raw Bar *Apalachicola, FL*

St. Joe Shrimp Company *Cape San Blas, FL*

Tasty Tails Seafood *Biloxi, MS*

Ted Peters Famous Smoked Fish *St. Petersburg, FL*

Thorny Oyster *Bay Saint Louis, MS*

Von's Bistro *Mobile, AL*

Walt'z Fish Shak *Madeira Beach, FL*

Westwego Shrimp Lot *Westwego, LA*

Wintzell's Oyster House *Mobile, AL*

FISHING GEAR & OUTFITTERS

239 Flies *Bonita Springs, FL*

Alabama Outdoors *Mobile, AL*

AMI Outfitters *Anna Maria Island, FL*

Angler 360 *Oldsmar, FL*

Apalach Outfitters *Apalachicola, FL*

Bill Jackson's Shop for Adventure *Pinellas Park, FL*

Bluewater Outriggers *Port St. Joe, FL*

Boaters Republic *Fort Myers, FL*

Boca Grande Outfitters *Boca Grande, FL*

BOTE *Grayton Beach, FL*

Chandeleur Outfitters *Ocean Springs, MS*

The Church Mouse *Fairhope, AL*

Coastal Outfitters *Daphne, AL*

Economy Tackle *Sarasota, FL*

Fisherman's Choice *Eastpoint, FL*

Flint Creek Outfitters *Dade City, FL*

Half Hitch *Navarre, FL*

Island Discount Tackle *Bradenton Beach, FL*

Island Outfitters *St. George Island, FL*

Lee Fisher International *Tampa, FL*

Mangrove Outfitters *Naples, FL*

Massey's Professional Outfitters *New Orleans, LA*

Nelson Outdoors *Pascagoula, MS*

Norm Zeigler's Fly Shop *Sanibel Island, FL*

Old Florida Outfitters *Santa Rosa Beach, FL*

On the Fly *Tampa, FL*

Orvis *Sandestin, FL*

Pack & Paddle *Lafayette, LA*

Red Beard's Outfitter *Mobile, AL*

The Rod Room *Orange Beach, AL*

Sea 2 Swamp Outfitters *Gautier, MS*

Sodium Fishing Gear *Crystal River, FL*

The South Outfitters *Pensacola, FL*

St. Pete Fishing Outfitters *St. Petersburg, FL*

Tailwater Outfitters *Palm Harbor, FL*

Tampa Bay Outfitters *Tampa, FL*

Tampa Fishing Outfitters *Tampa, FL*

Whidden's Marina *Boca Grande, FL*

Whitney's Bait & Tackle *Sanibel Island, FL*

Yellowfin Ocean Sports *Santa Rosa Beach, FL*

INDEX